# I See Things

Ric Eittreim

## Contact and Copyright Information



ISBN: 979-8-9889491-9-0 (paperback)
ISBN: 979-8-9889491-7-6 (ebook)

## Images and Artwork

All images included in this book are the exclusive property of the author.

With the single exception of the public domain image of "*young/old woman*", no other images used in this book are from any other source, public or private.

---

All artwork was created by the author and is whimsical by design.

No attempt has been made to mimic any public or private individuals, places or things and all images are solely for entertainment and not intended to offend, annoy or harass anyone in any way, shape or form.

For information regarding reprints or rights to this material, please contact the author at the following email.

**Contact: rice@northidahomedia.com NorthIdahoMedia.com**

# Dedications

Writing a book, even one as seemingly simple as "I See Things", is not an easy task. So many things to consider about font style and size, when to use italics, how to insert the images. The overall layout, artwork, look and feel. Then creating the content!

Now with a draft in hand, where are the mistakes? I'm sure they are in here somewhere. The point is, it's just not possible to create a book without asking other people for help. We really arc a social lot and when it comes to creating whimsical works, we need each other even more. "*Does this look ok to you", "Can you understand what I"m trying to convey here?*", and so on. Having friends and family help along this journey is very much a blessing and is sincerely appreciated.

So…Thanks to Elizabeth my darling wife for first of all, helping me with colors and my lame attempt at artwork. Having your input has been comforting and immensely helpful. Not to mention putting up with my somewhat annoying habit of getting focused at the expense of missing the rest of life around me.

I want to also mention a good friend and mentor that we lost a couple of years ago. Al S. was a major influence in my life and hc brought total joy and fascination into my life as well as a deep appreciation for the more whimsical side of life. Al was that rare person that could understand complex business situations and in the next moment move into an imaginary state that few could rival. He was a unique and fascinating individual. He would have loved seeing this book.

And to my writer friends – self published and those with major publishing contracts – Hats off to Jon, Chuck, Monte, David, Mark, Richard and all the others that have suggested that I write a book. This is not the book you thought you would see me write – but it's a start :-)

And for those that actually read this book – a heartfelt thank you for taking the time to have a look. I hope your life is full of whimsy and beauty.

Ric – March, 2023

# What is This Book About?

## Whimsical Perceptions of Everyday Life.

This is a book about how we perceive things. Since I wrote this book I suppose you could say this is about how "I" perceive things… but I have spoken with many people on this topic so I'm fairly certain that while viewing something that many people have also experienced a fascinating "transformation" of *things into other things.*

This story is about what happens in my mind when I see a landscape, a cloud, a rock or tree. And while looking at that scene, a new object may magically appear in the form of a face, animal or something else.

Sometimes, objects can take on the most amazing transformation…

As you view the following pages, you will see a picture like this snow covered rock (to the right), then the same picture but with what I also saw is drawn into the picture (below.)

That new "thing" that I saw is drawn over the top of the original picture – like the smiling goofball rock below.

By showing the original picture followed by the edited picture, I can share with you what I saw in that scene.

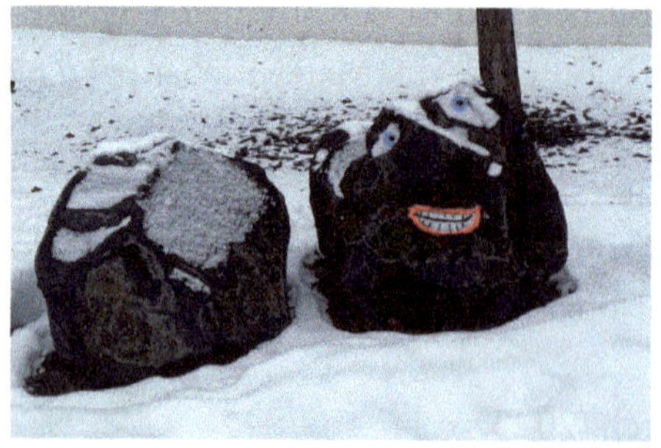

*Fun? Interesting?*
*I sure hope so…*

# Why This Book

**My point of view:** My brain seems to run overtime with respect to seeing objects turn into other things. I have a hard time looking anywhere without seeing a tree turn into a creature of some sort. On a beach in California, I turned to face away from the ocean – as I viewed the cliff above the beach, many shapes in the cliff came to life; a Labrador dog, an old Indian face outline, a whale, a seal, a goofy alien face… they all appeared in an instant. This visual morphing happens to me all the time – it's hard to even look at a cedar tree without my mind turning the branches into schnauzers (dogs with the coolest mustaches)

An interesting question – what to do with this image creating brain of mine? I See Things is a natural outlet for me to share with you what happens to me in my daily cacophony of mind-numbing imagery.

**Reader point of view:** As you read along, see what happens in your brain as you view the original images. Do you see faces? The head of a dog? That ancient Indian looking out over the ocean waters? Let's see if your brain is just as interested as mine seems to be in bringing all these wonderful creatures to life…

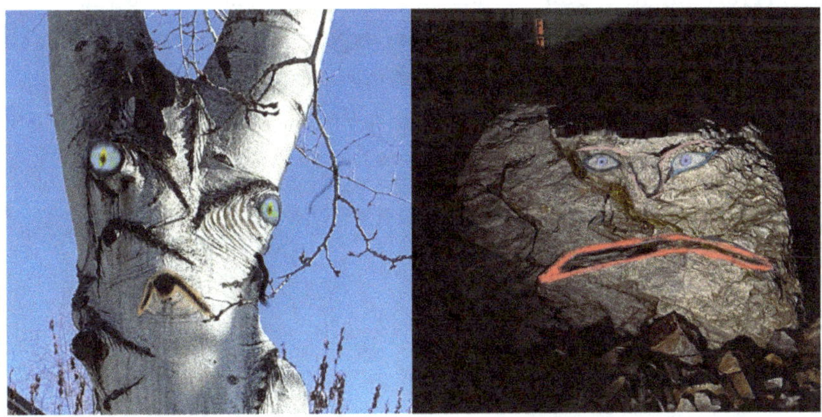

We have all heard the expression, "*when a tree falls in the woods and no people are nearby, does it make a sound?*" Well, when we gaze upon the many objects around us, "*do they live if we are not looking at them?*"

# So...

*Please join me for a look into the quirky soul of nature as experienced from the mind of a person who sees the world through color-blind eyes, a creative mind, and a very whimsical outlook on life.*

---

First, let's accept this point... *Many people see faces in objects as they look around at everyday things.*

I think it's fair to say that many of us see "things" in other "things." How many times has this happened to you? Or a friend mentioned, "look at that cloud – it looks like a rabbit! (or whatever!)" – this odd vision – shifted view seems to happen to many of us.

Think about it – A cloud appears in the shape of a bird. Maybe the cloud looks more like an angel or a dog... it's not unusual to see clouds appear in the shapes of familiar objects. Even a tree or a rock can turn into the most amazing creature – maybe that old log along side of a hiking trail turns into a seal or whale. A rock might appear like the face of an old Indian chief or maybe it has the outline of a Labrador dog. We all have experienced moments like this when right before our eyes, objects have turned into creatures and other things.

*Can you see a wispy old man with a curling beard looking to the left? What about the creature looking down... eyes and nose? Do you see it?*

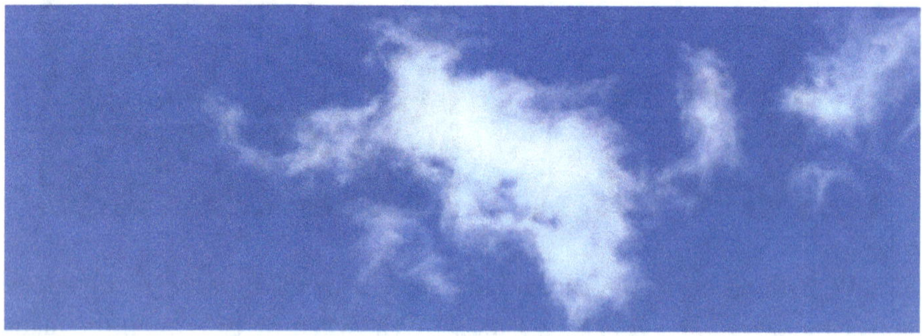

# How to Read This Book

Those pages with a single image are; original image page first, then the edited page version with my "artwork." Pages that have two images; the top image is the original unedited image. That is the object as it appears in the real world. Look at that image to see what "pops" out for you. This is where you should spend some time to allow your brain to find or create a face or object *(or two or three!)*

*Original Image is at the top of the page*

The bottom image on two-image pages will have my interpretation of the image along with the added "personality" drawn by the author. And please remember that my drawing skills are limited, at best.

*This is a book about perception, not about artwork.*

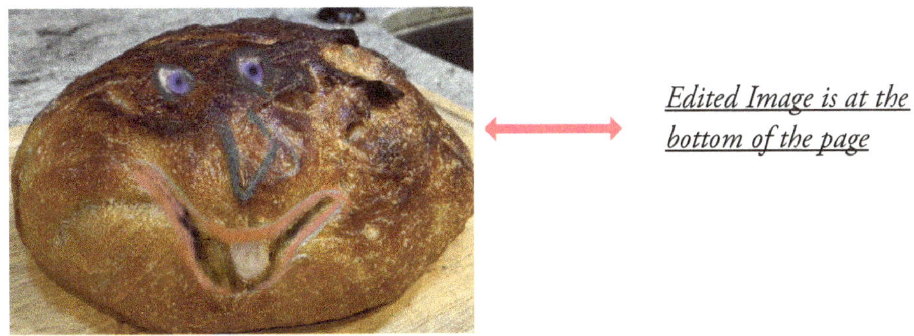

*Edited Image is at the bottom of the page*

# Apple Pie Crust

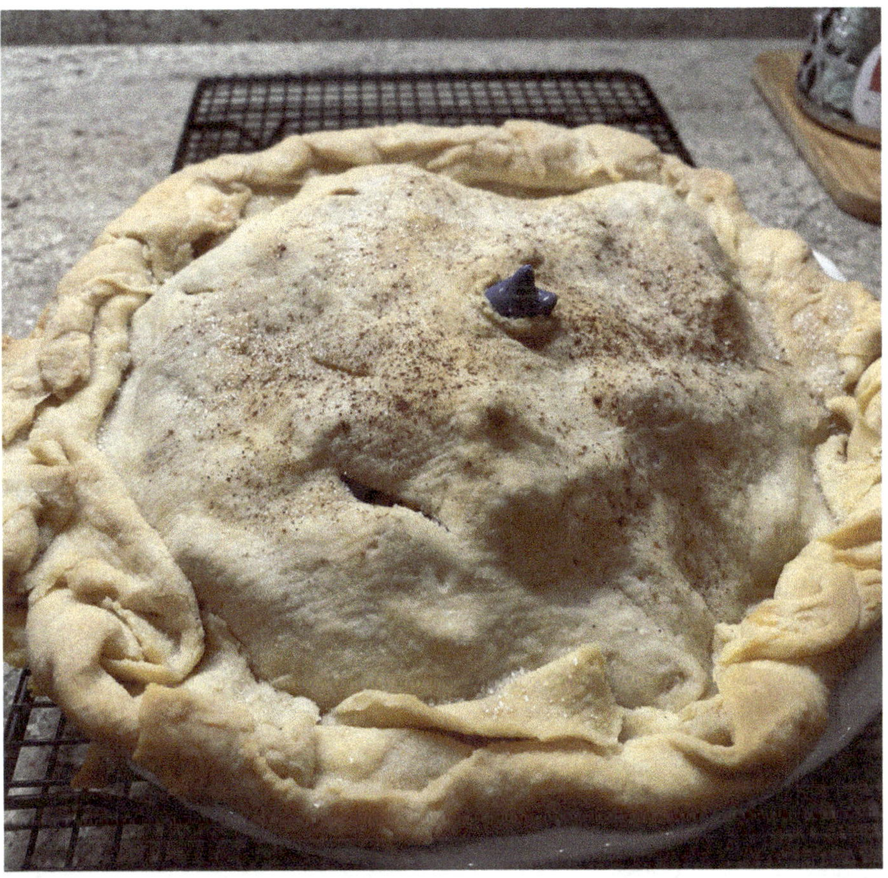

If you are wondering what the right eye has in it, that's a "Pie Bird" – these are ceramic shapes (this one a bird) that are hollow to allow steam to escape while baking.

So, how's this for a good looking apple pie. I have to say, it was delicious :-) But do you see the face in this crust?

# Pie-face

Pie crust can turn out so many different ways – this one had a couple of eyes and that goofy sort of smile look to it. I could not help myself and had to add the face drawing.

Now, go back to the original image. See it? And, I have to admit it – we did eat the pie. And it was really good!

*Hey, not only are you discovering more about perception, you just learned a baking tip about how to use a pie bird!*

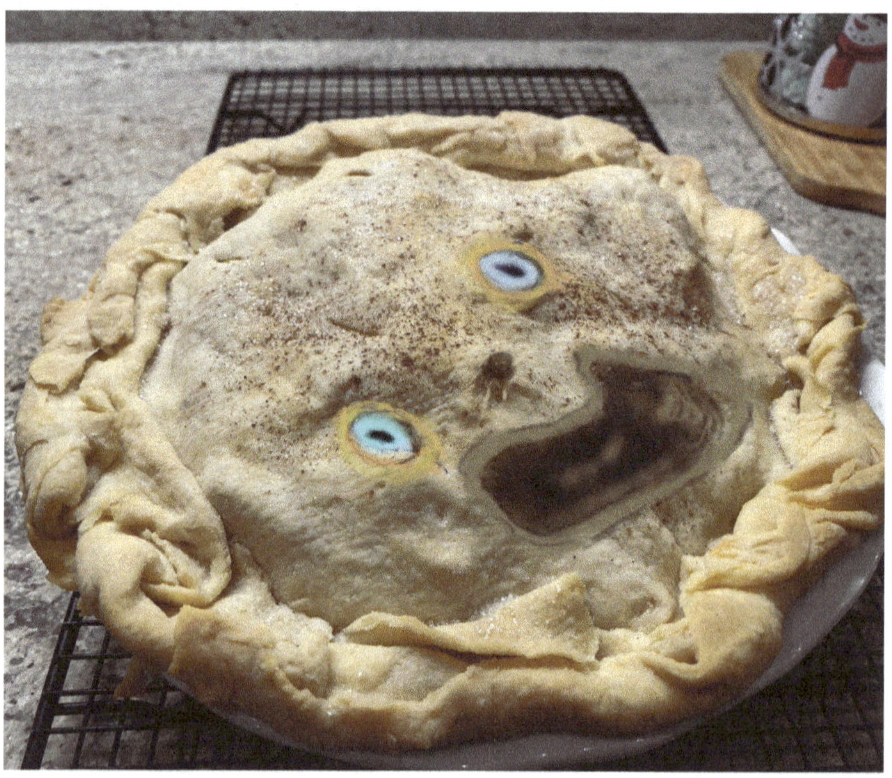

# The Tree Face

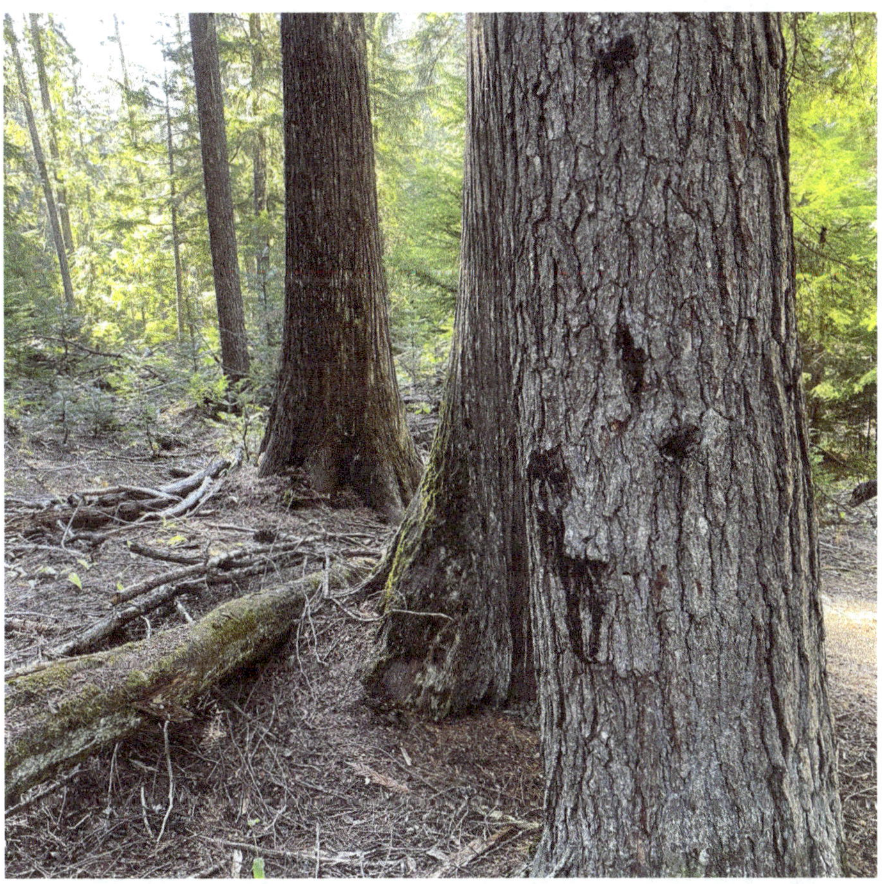

It really is amazing that certain trees do not need much help to turn into some form of a face. Someone had spent a bit of time giving this tree a few whacks with a tool.

I think this tree was well on its way to coming alive without the help of my incredible art skills :-)

# Long Tooth

It's not clear how the bark gets mangled on these trees but given they are next to a popular campground, we can make a guess that visitors wield the old camp axe or hatchet and gave the nearby trees a whack or two.

To clearly illustrate my point about seeing a face, I did choose to color in ways that certainly would not be natural. But then again, I guess nothing I'm doing here would occur in nature…

This guy almost looks like he's about to say, "duh!"

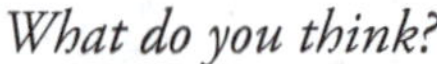

*What do you think?*

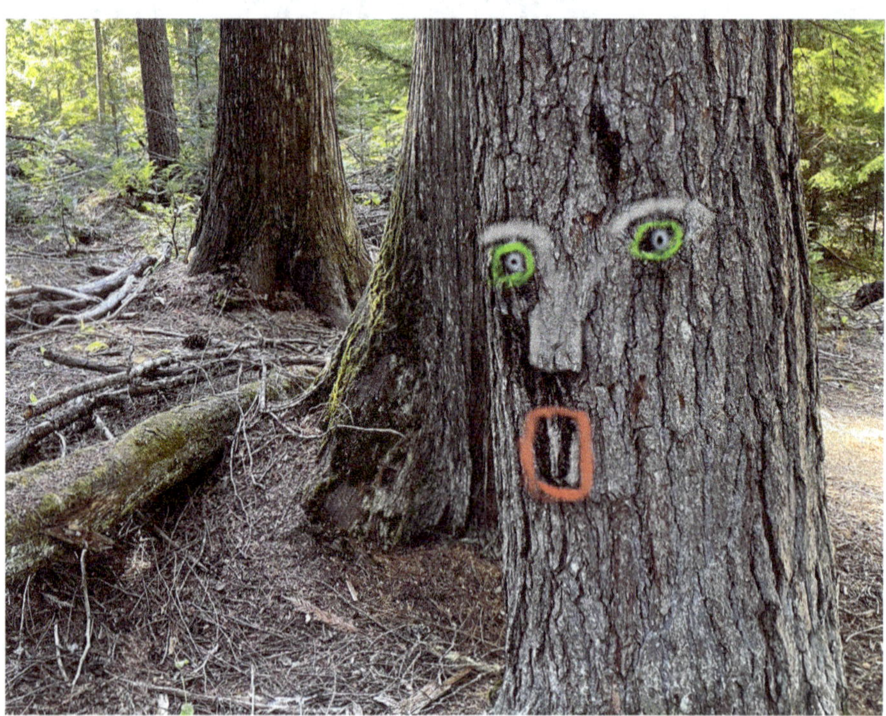

# Sourdough

I think everyone loves the smell of bread just coming out of the oven. Cooking sourdough has been a project of mine for the past couple of years. During a trip to visit family in Colorado, they had been baking loaves of sourdough bread and I learned about the starter, feeding the starter and the process of making a sourdough loaf of bread.

Of course I was interested in the process so we came home to North Idaho with a cup of high mountain Colorado sourdough starter.

And I needed a couple of loaves so I would be able to write this book (ok, just kidding....)

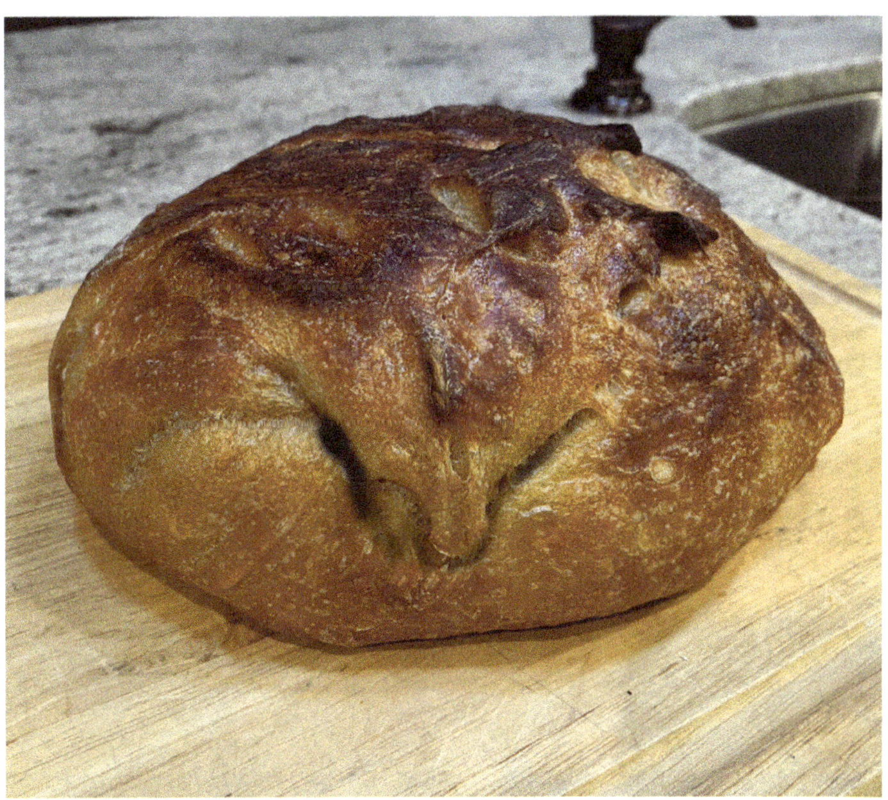

# Sourpuss

With a lip that hangs that low, this guy is really putting on a show. The crust on sourdough bread always comes out different and always has some "crusty" old form to it.

If this loafer could talk, I wonder what he would be saying? Maybe telling the rest of us, *"Hey, quit loafing around!", "How much dough do you have?", "Hey, can you spare a little bread?", "Look at all these bumps in my crust, how lame*[1] *is that?"*

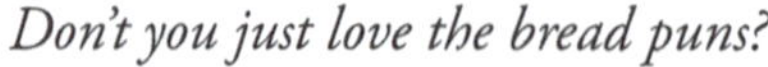

*Don't you just love the bread puns?*

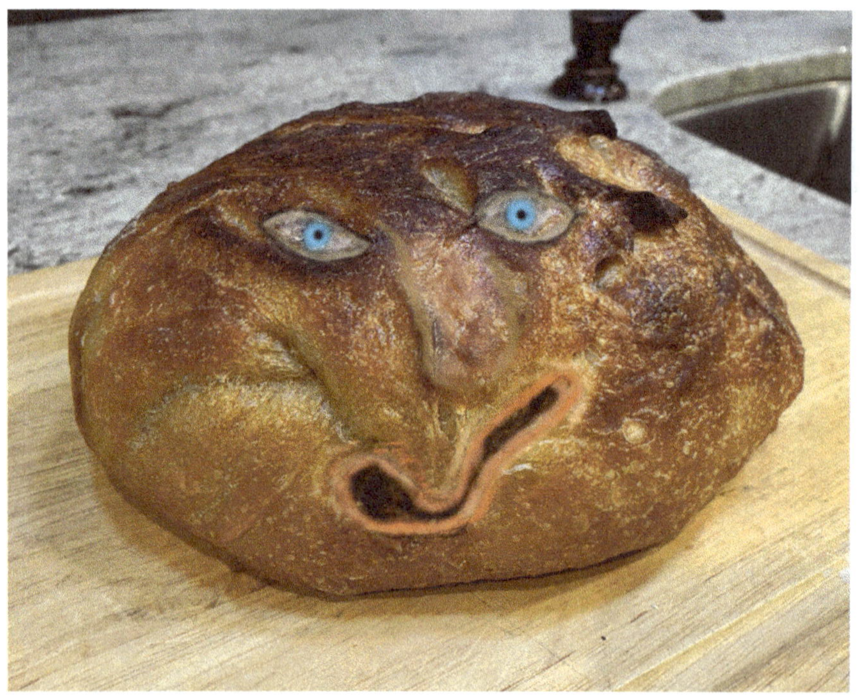

---

[1] Lame; A Lame (pronounced LAHM, meaning "blade" in French) is typically a long thin stick made to hold a metal razor used to cut, or score, bread dough to help control the expansion of the loaf as it bakes.

# The Old Cottonwood

We were staying at the Century Campground in Salmon, Idaho *(new owner in 2022; changed the name to "Andreas on the River".)* Great place to visit – the campground is right in the town of Salmon and about a 5 minute walk to the Odd Fellows Bakery. Let me tell you, if you like croissants, then stop here. They make incredibly good ones – especially their breakfast version. Also some great breads.

So, this gnarly old tree keep calling me. I'm pretty sure this is a cottonwood and it's about 50 feet from the Salmon River.

We were parked a little way behind this tree – imagine my surprise when I walked around the tree and saw this! Can you see the face?

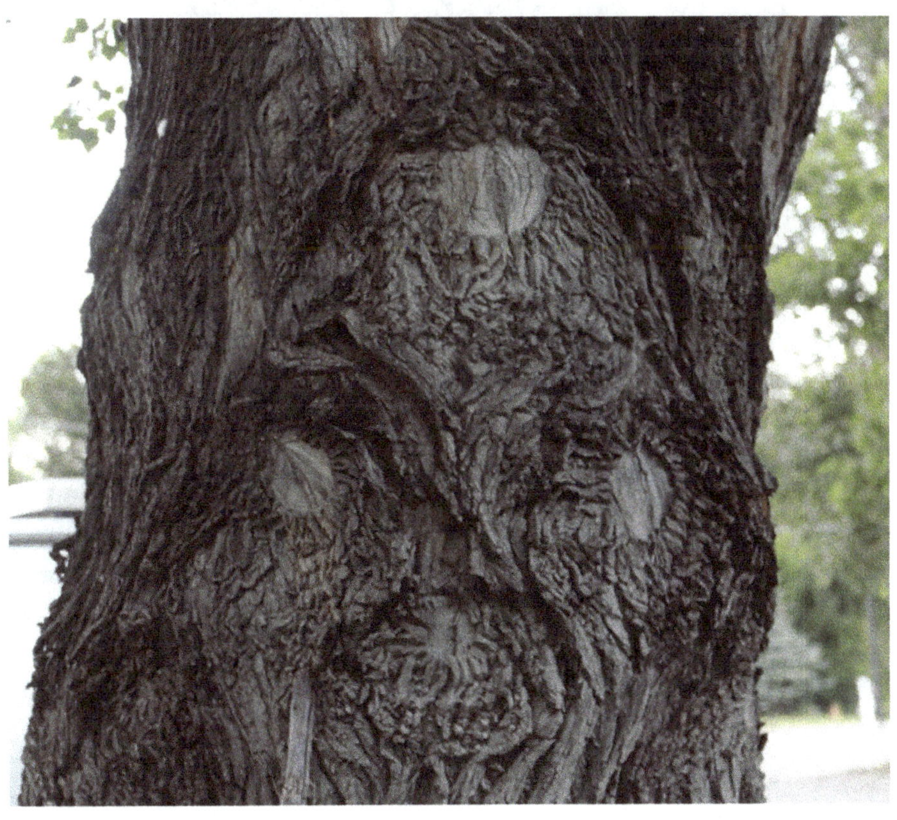

# Old 3 Eye

Old 3-eye was waiting and watching to make sure we did not harm any of his tree flock… we were good! Did not want to upset this guy.

I have no idea how old this tree is – certainly has become a bit gnarly over the years. Cottonwoods love water and tend to grow in wet areas like wetlands and areas near a stream or lake.

Perhaps that look is from the cold Idaho winters. Or maybe it's just an old tree with an attitude…

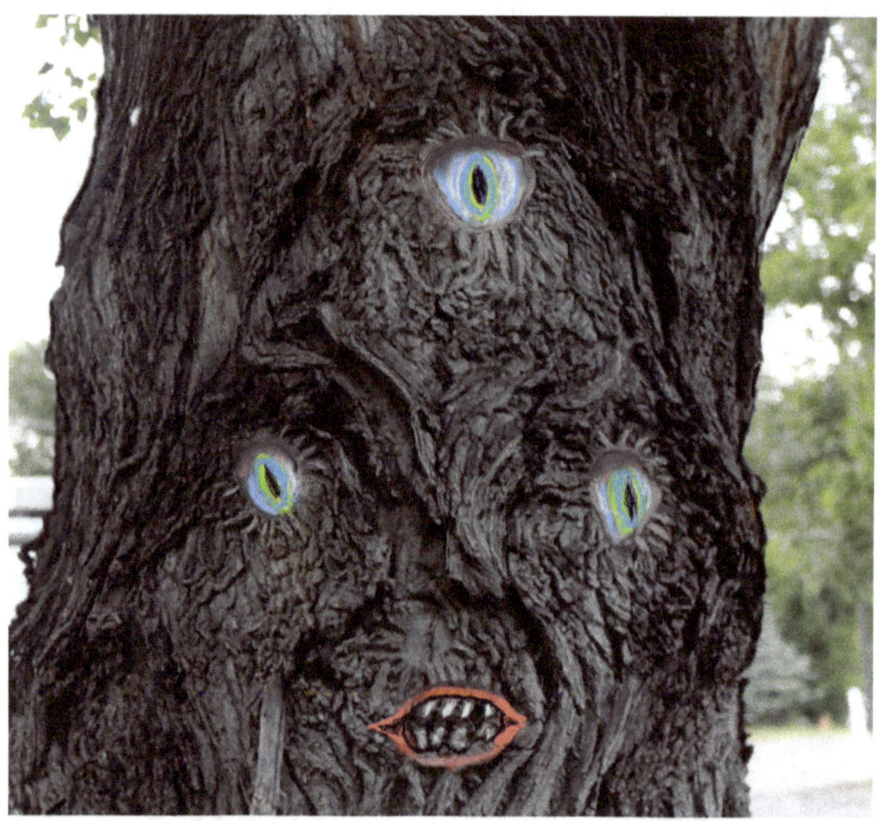

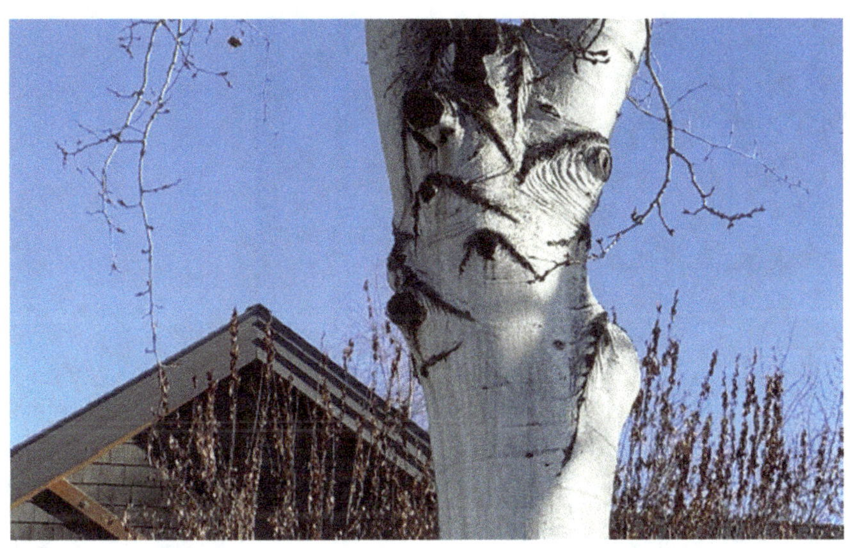

## Tree Snail

This tree took on a life of its own… Those eyes were following our every step as we carefully walked past!

I think this is sort of like a tree version of a snail… what do you think it looks like?

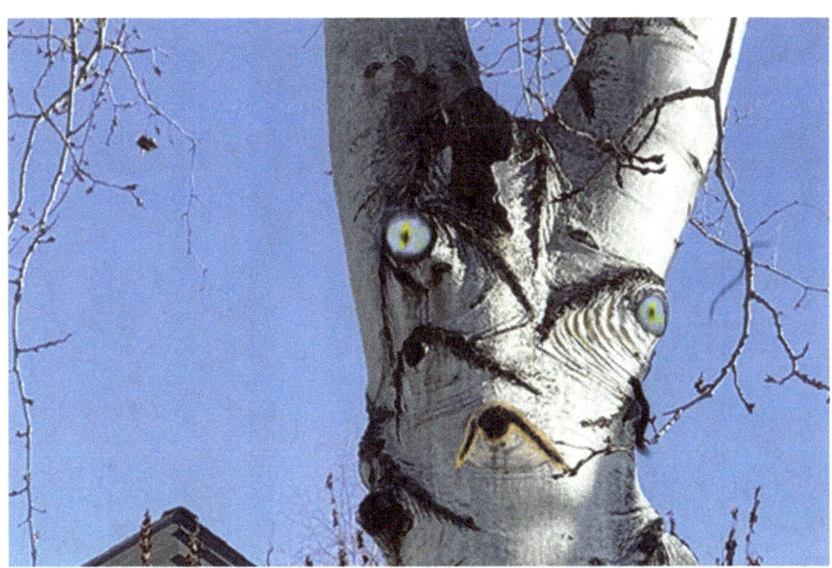

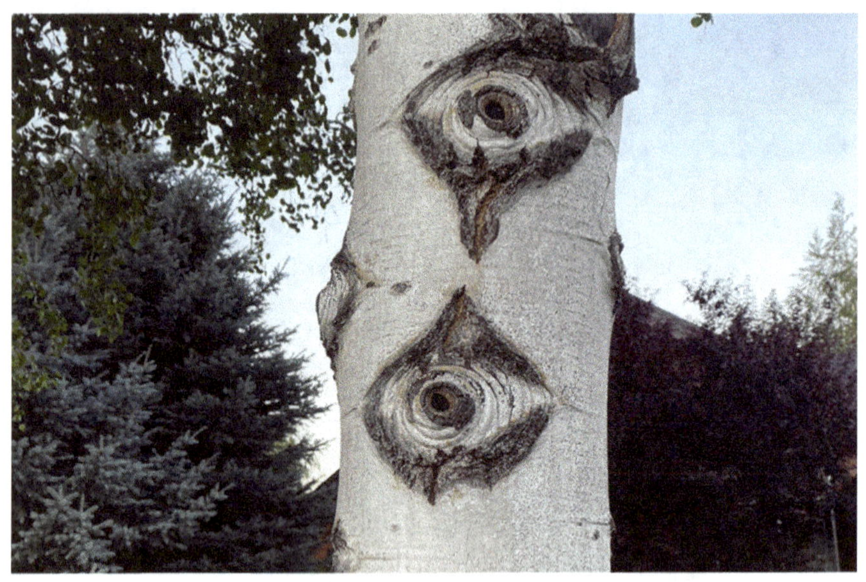

# Eye Stack

What on earth is living in our neighborhood? This tree sort of took on a life of its own… We might think the best way to orient ourselves is to have both eyes on the same plane but hey, this guy is ok stacking the eyes.

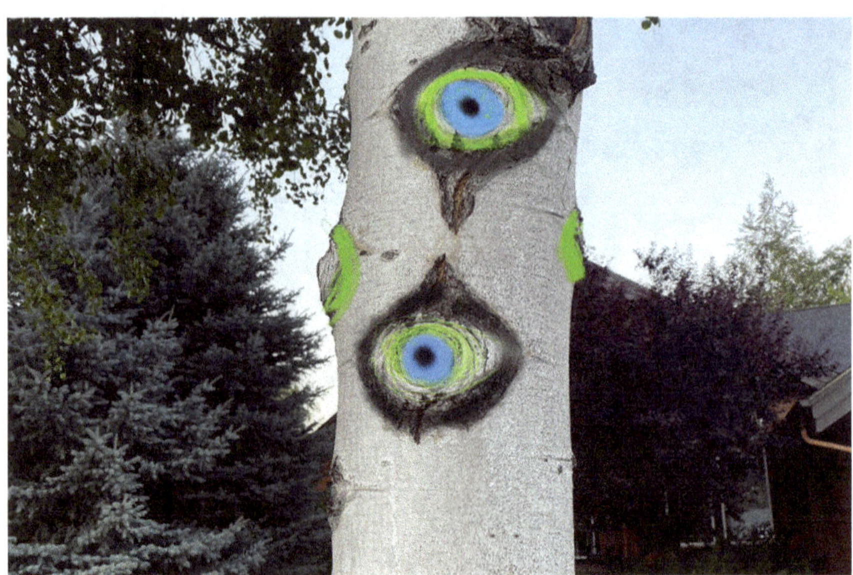

# Copper Falls

In North Idaho, about a mile from the Canadian border is a beautiful little waterfall named, "Copper Falls."

We often camp nearby and have visited this waterfall many times. This area is home to both black and grizzly bear so it's a place where we are very careful.

We were standing and enjoying the falls one day. What caught my eye was the dark areas behind the water that appeared to be like eyes... So of course, it's part of this book. How could I resist?

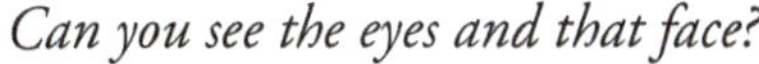

*Can you see the eyes and that face?*

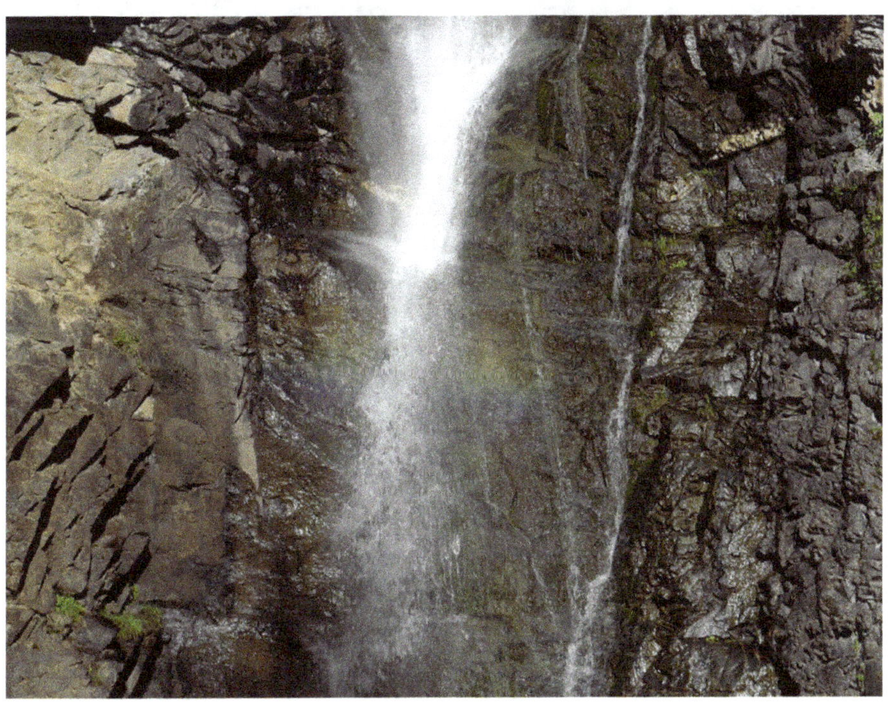

# Copper Face

Well, these are the “eyes” and this is the face behind Copper Falls that I mentioned. Did you see this image in the original picture? If you look back at the original now, can you “unsee” that face? Pretty crazy what happens.

*And what about the other faces? Did you find them?*

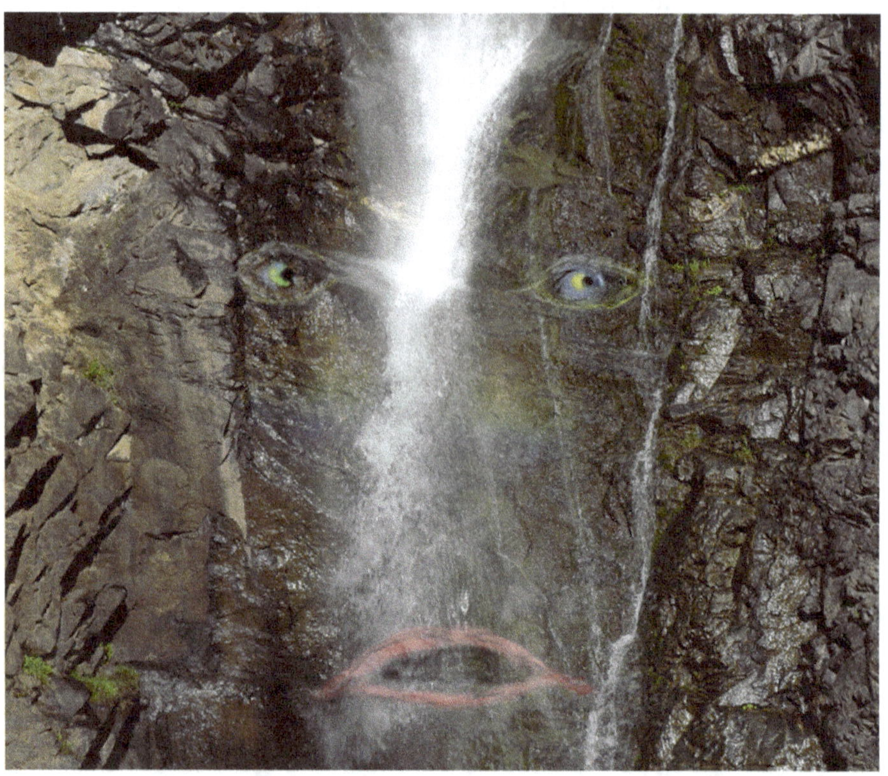

# More, More, More

Did you see all of these? Go back and forth and see if you end up finding the same ones that I did.

Next time you are out in the woods or even downtown in a city – look around you and see how many times you see a "face" in a cliff, a building or in the landscape.

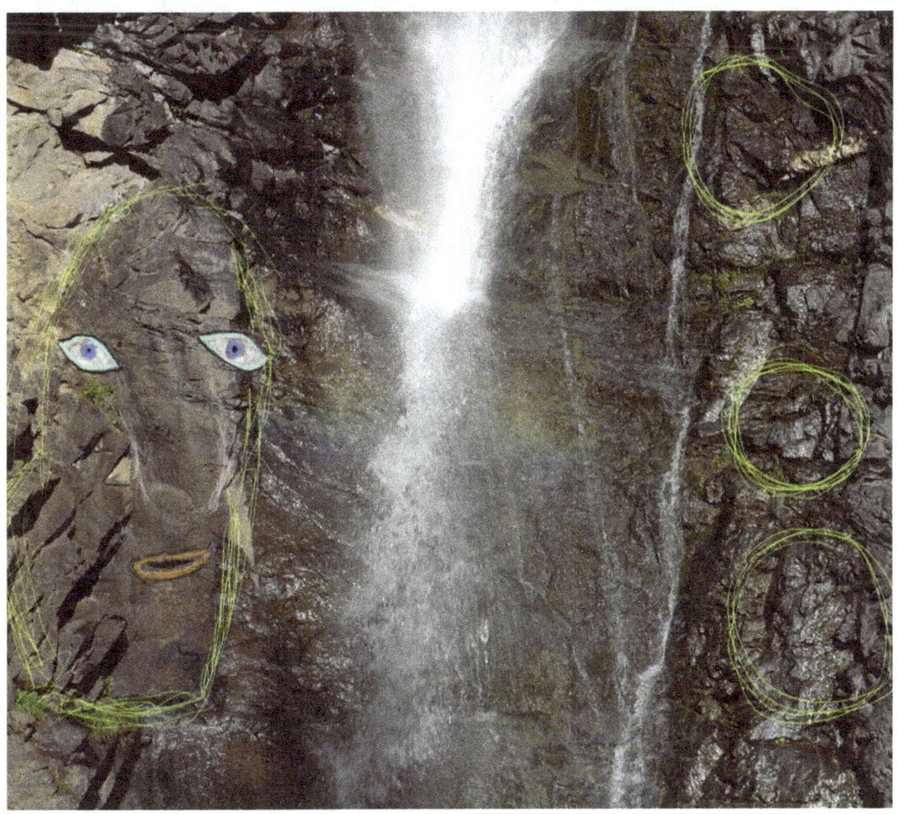

# Ross Creek Cedars

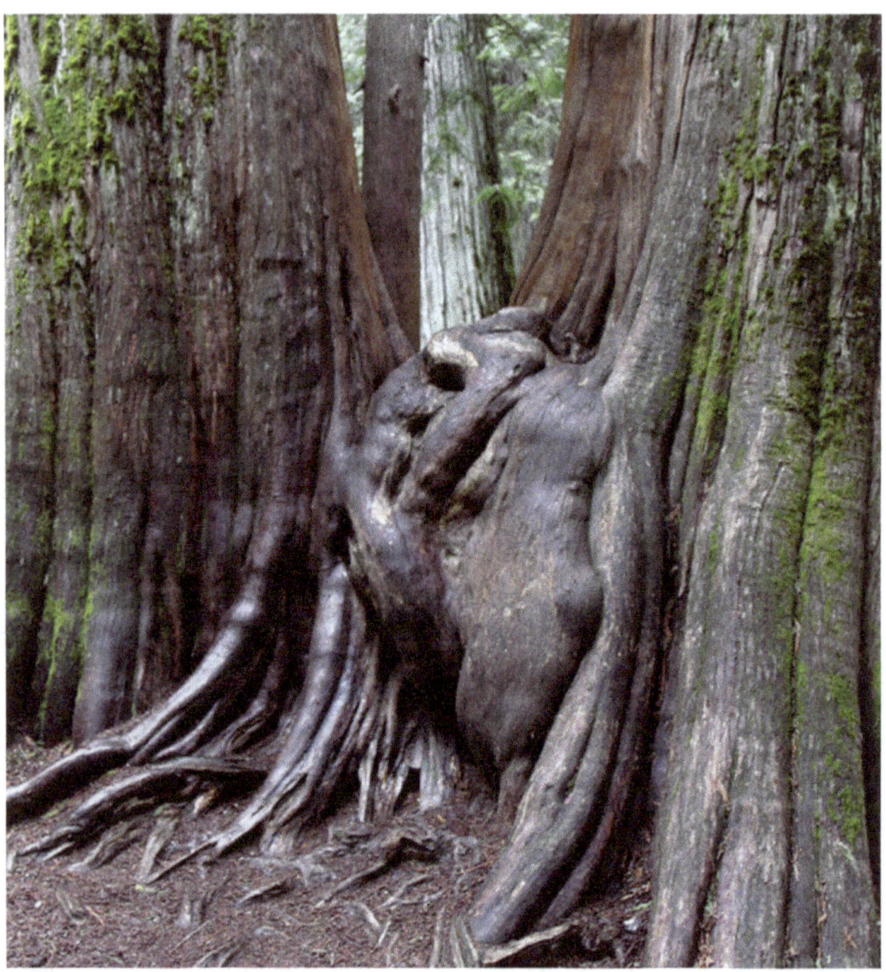

Ross Creek Cedars near Libby, Montana. This is one special and beautiful place. The old growth cedars are spectacular and well worth visiting. This picture does not do justice to the magnificent grove of cedars so look it up and visit if you get the opportunity.

*Why does this remind me of a sci-fi movie creature...*

# Tree Alien

Walking along a trail in the grove at Ross Creek Cedars, a tree leech appeared. Or tree alien or whatever. Or maybe this is a long lost relative of some large snail-like movie creature?

This creature was certainly hugging tight onto that tree. Perhaps this strange woody creature was making sure we were behaving ourselves?

*Whatever it was, we kept walking...*

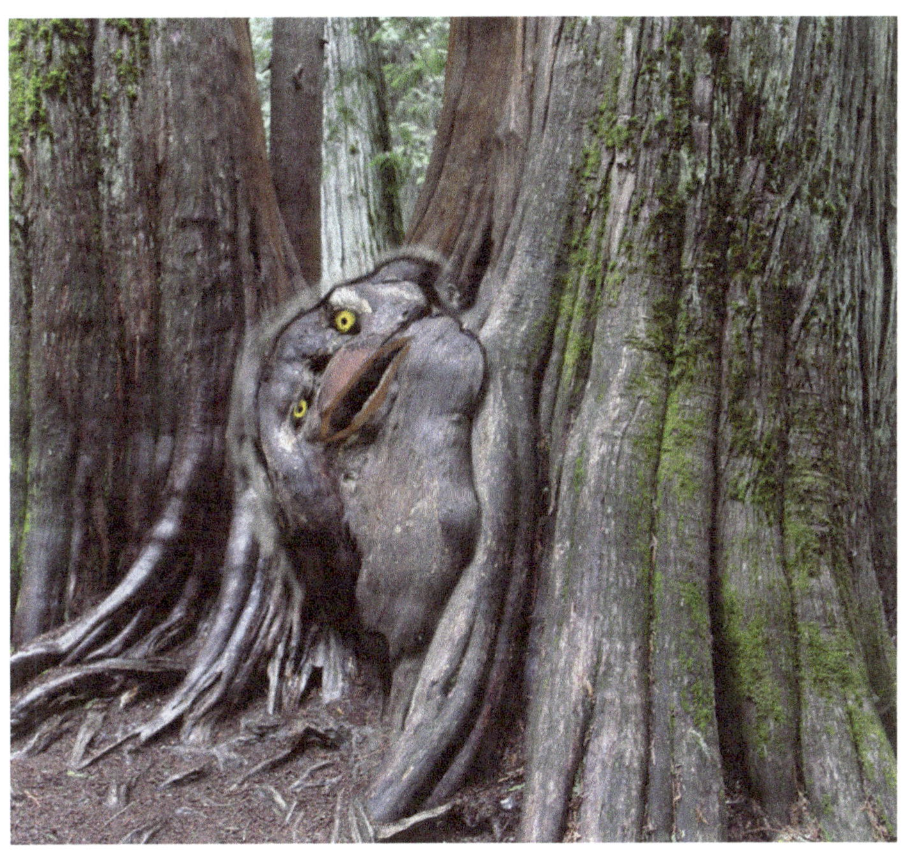

# Old Stoneface

This old rock is a "stones throw" from my front door. We often walk past this location while walking our chocolate lab puppy. Well, at 20 months, maybe not so much a puppy still but hey, it's a lab and they act like puppies for a few years.

The rock does have a frown, that's for sure. This lighting accented the rock so it took on a sort of scary feel. Or maybe just a bit crabby!

Can you see the face in this rock? I wonder if you will see this the same way as I have.

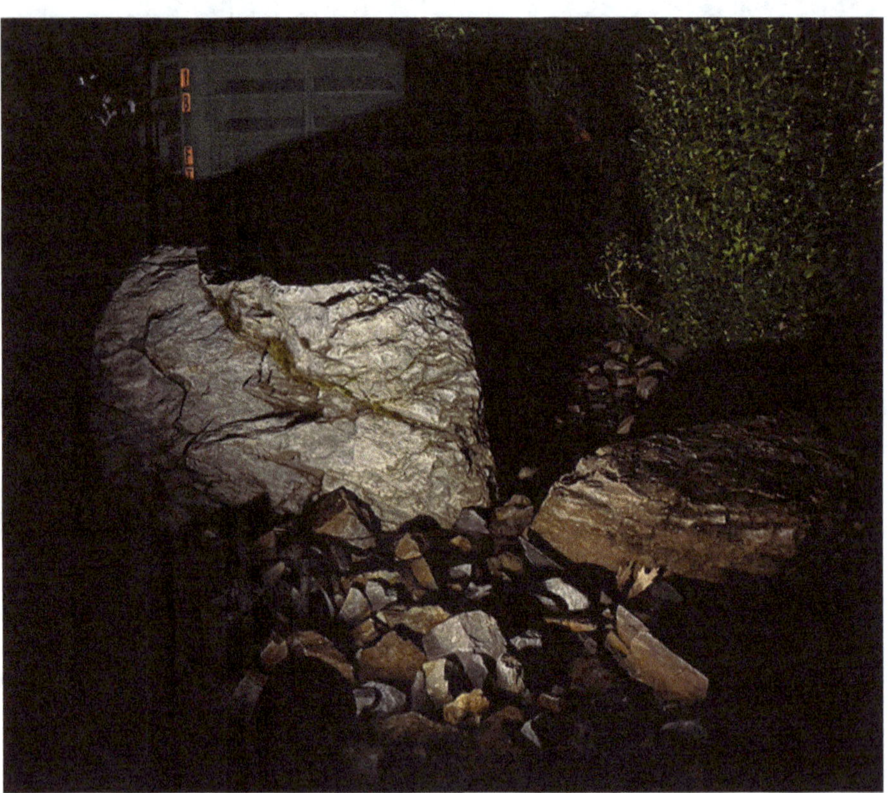

# Grumpy Stoneface

Talk about a face made of stone! This guy is made to scowl. That frown is frozen in place and I don't think it will ever smile.

And now that you "see" the face, look at the previous picture and try to "unsee[1]" that face!

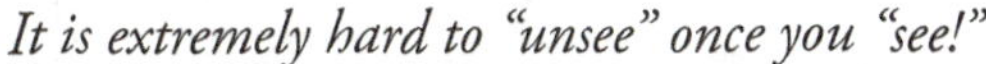

*It is extremely hard to "unsee" once you "see!"*

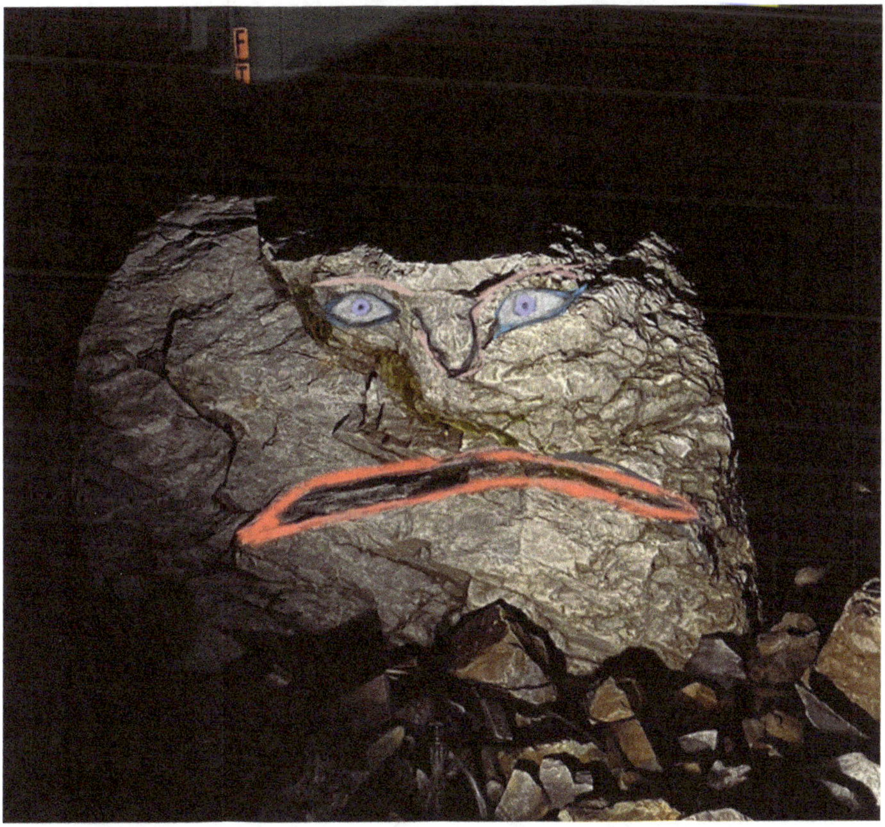

1 erase the memory of or no longer register (something unpleasant or distasteful that one has seen or noticed). "when you realize that she bleached her eyebrows, you really can't unsee it"

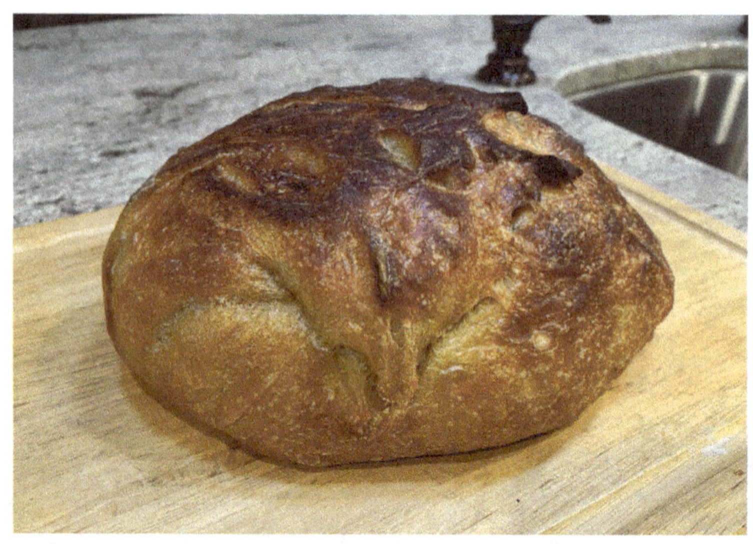

# Goofy Loaf

Oh, oh… someone has been baking sourdough bread again. And this one was just plain old wacky. Or goofy… both apply.

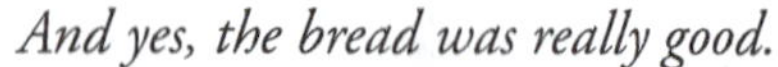

*And yes, the bread was really good.*

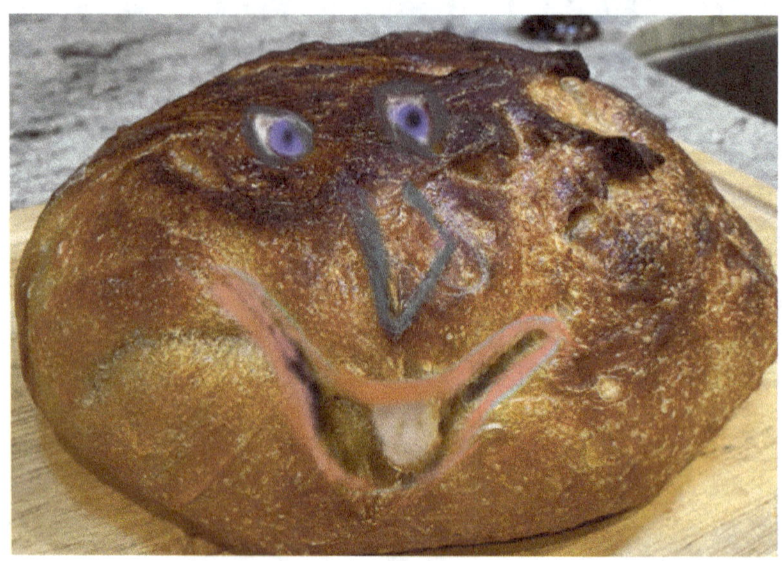

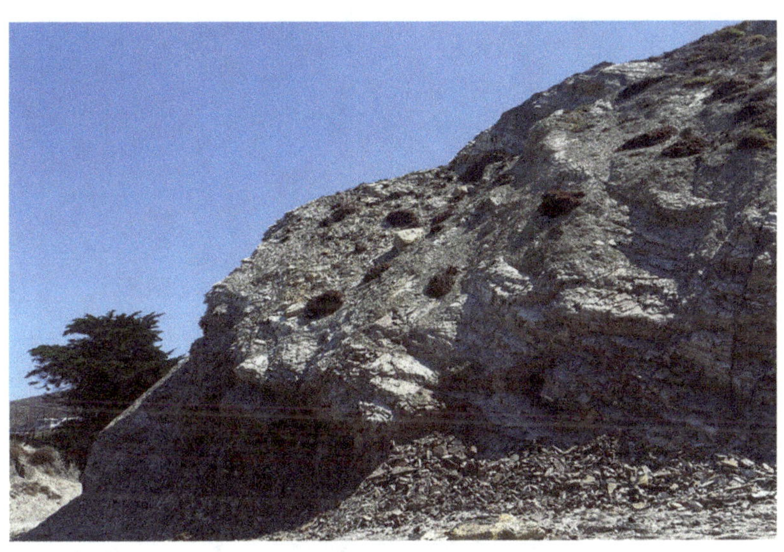

# Jalama Dragon

This guy was nose to the ground, looking out at the Pacific ocean on a warm day at Jalama Beach.

To me, this is sort of a cross between a leopard seal and maybe a cousin to Nessie the Loch Ness creature?

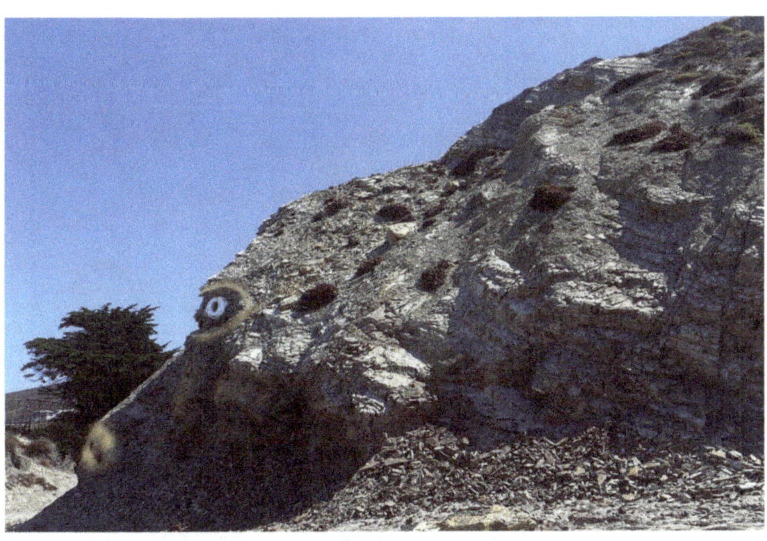

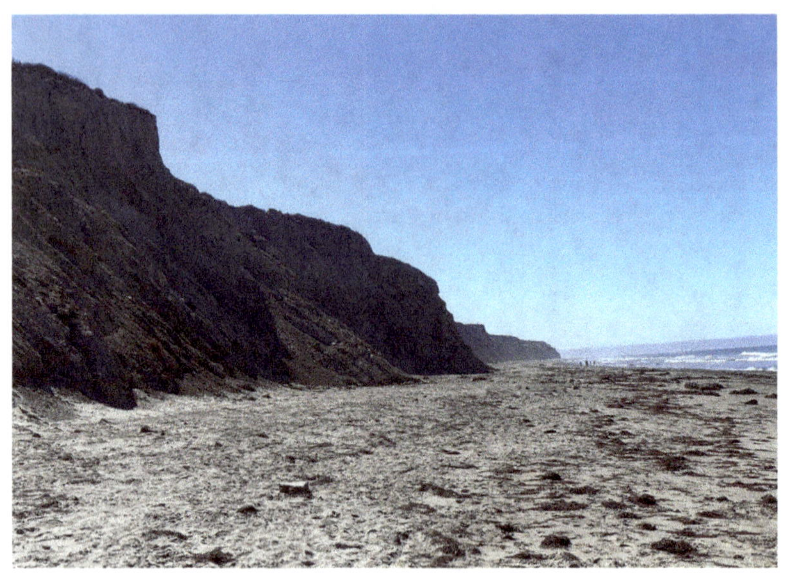

# Indian Spirit

Jalama Beach, California. A fun, sunny and non-windy day. The beach offered great weather so I ambled down the beach and managed to find the face of an ancient Chumash spirit. *Note: with all due respect to the Chumash – I love this beach a lot and highly respect your neighborhood and homeland.*

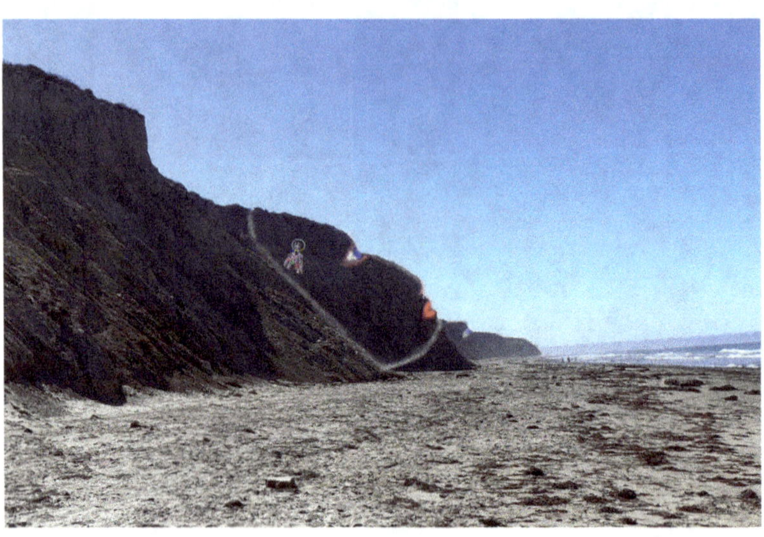

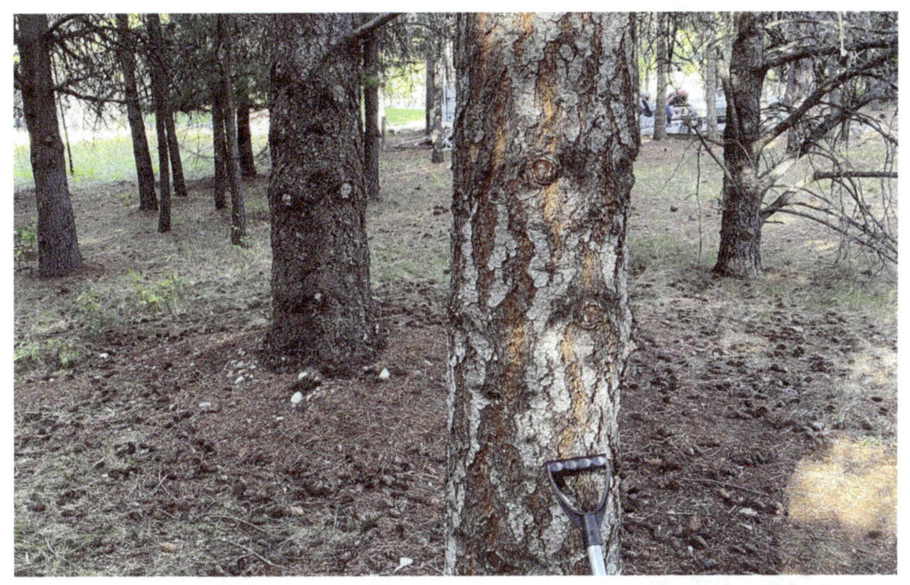

## Shovel Tree

So, we are out camping at Farragut State Park in North Idaho and I leaned our camp shovel on a tree. You can see the handle in the picture – but more importantly, do you see one creature or two creatures in this picture?

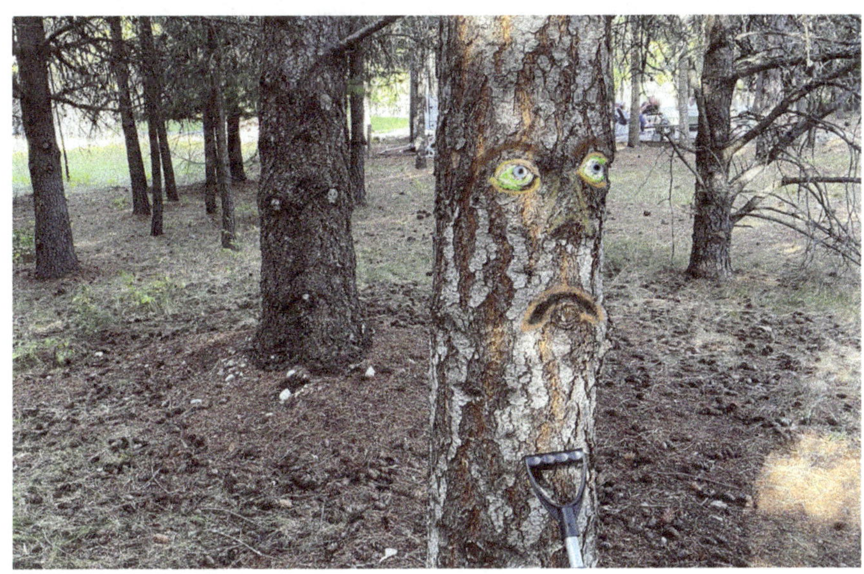

# Shovel Tree & Friend

Did you see that tree in the background? Pretty amazing how these things just pop out at us. Then, once you do see it, it's impossible to "unsee" the object!

So, I have added some fantastic artwork and now look behind the shovel tree… I can't tell you how many times I have looked at a picture and was surprised that other creatures show up.

*Looks like Shovel tree had a back up buddy!*

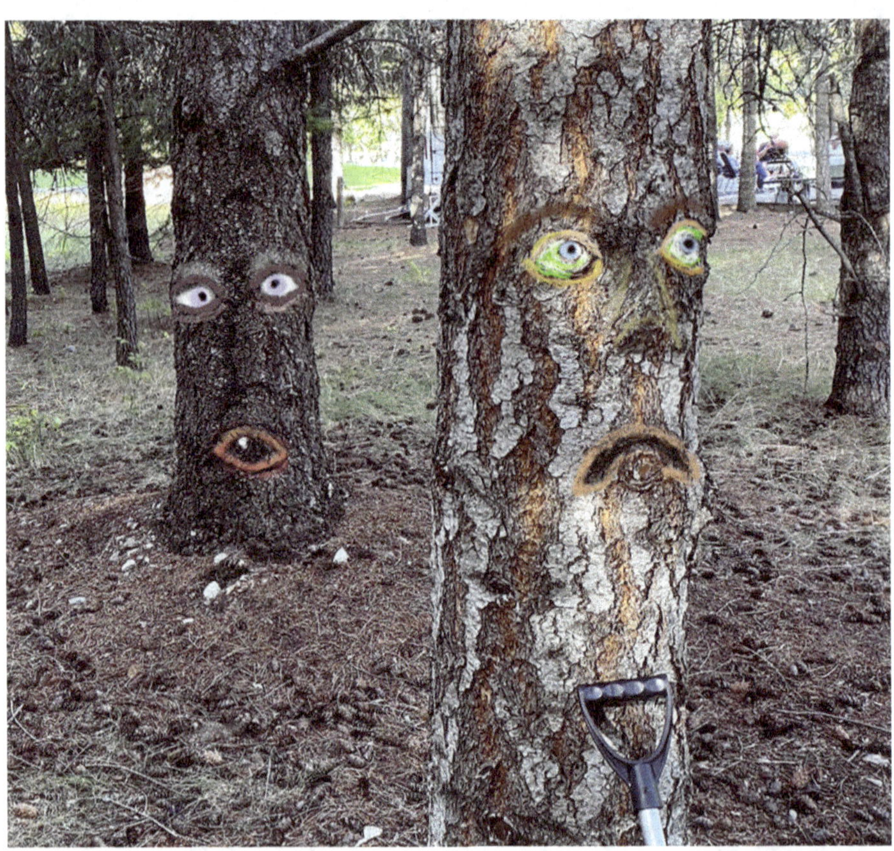

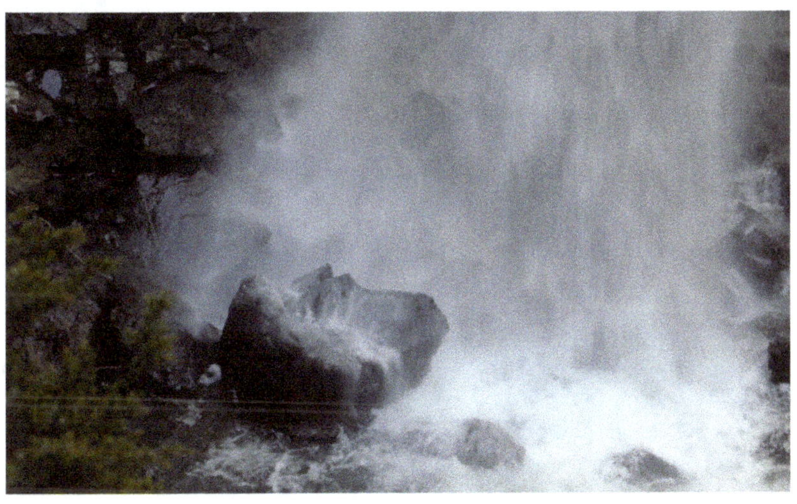

# Shower Rock

This rock is at the bottom of Copper Falls. This is a beautiful little waterfall in North Idaho, about a mile from the border with Canada. As I watched, that rock turned into a head and the face appeared in front of my eyes. At least it's a clean face with all that water!

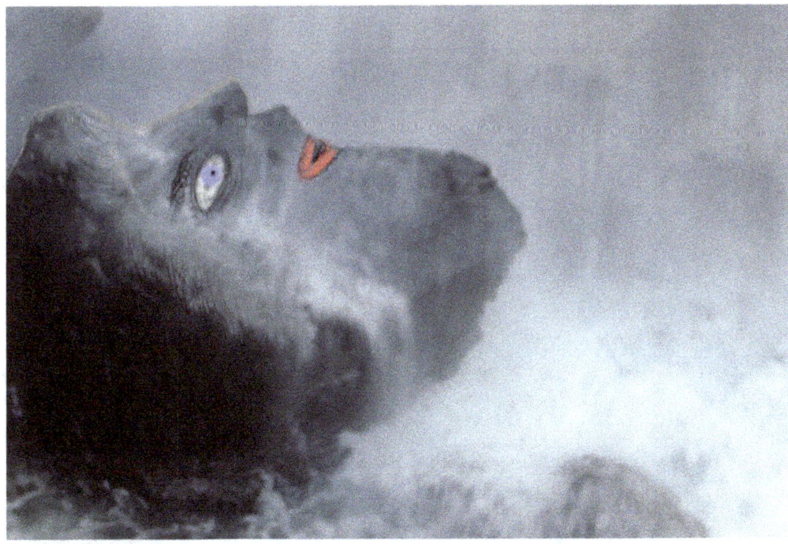

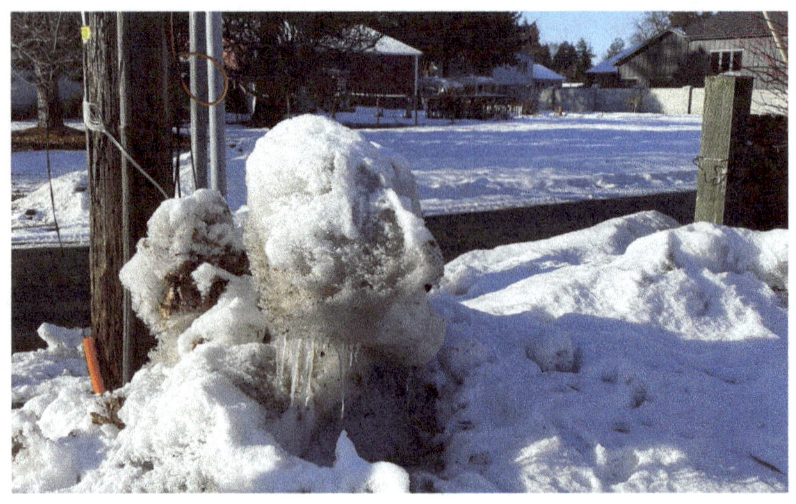

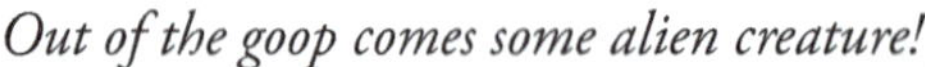

# This Is Snow Alien

This is one gritty looking snow creature. We had some warm days with a lot of snow melt and all the road slush combined to turn the fresh white snow into a muddy slushy goop.

*Out of the goop comes some alien creature!*

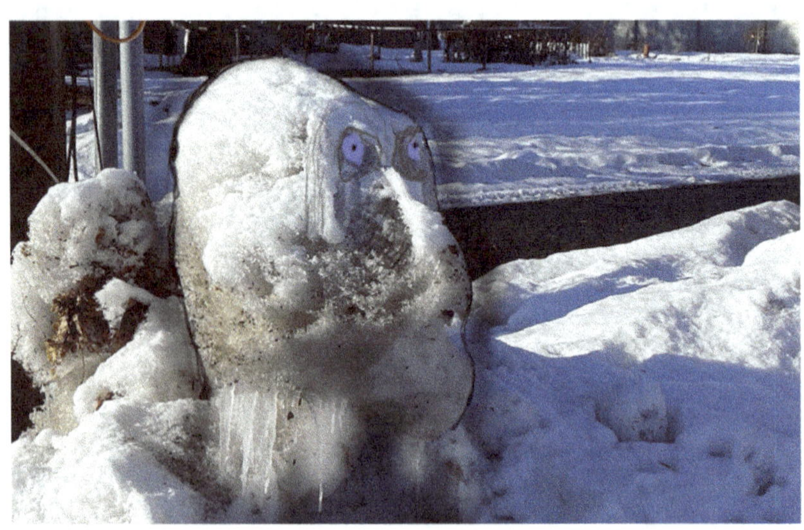

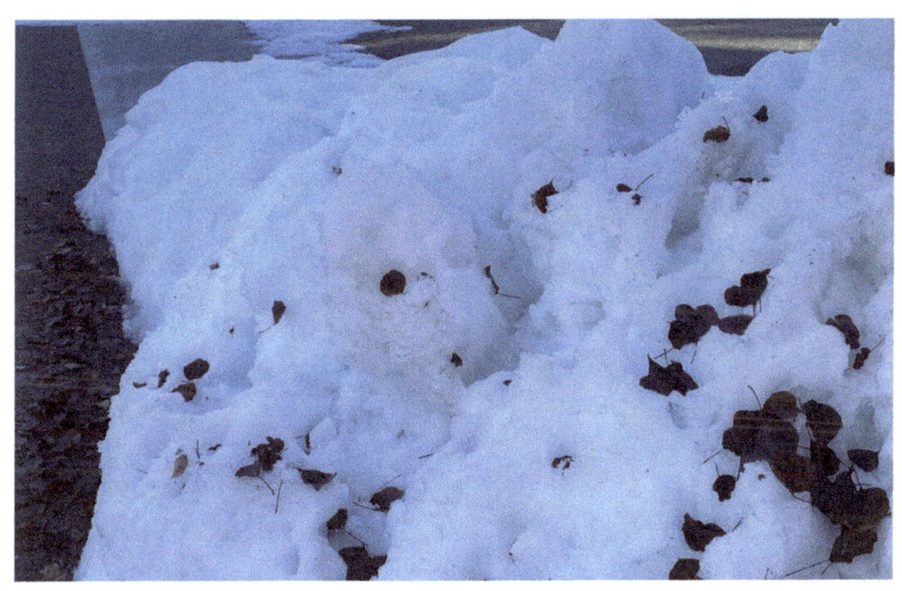

## The Puppy

'Come on... who does not love a warm puppy? Well, maybe this not very warm but hey – you see the pup? Right?

Now look again at the top picture!

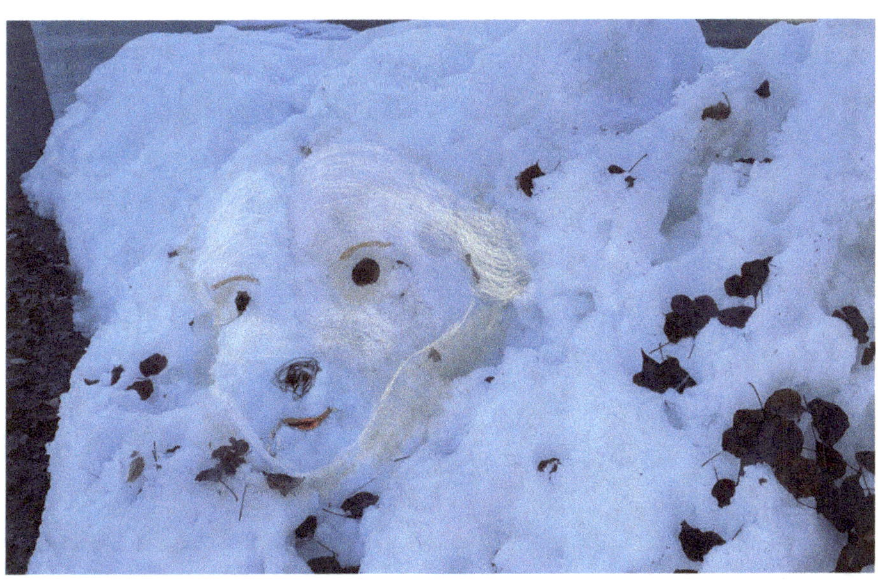

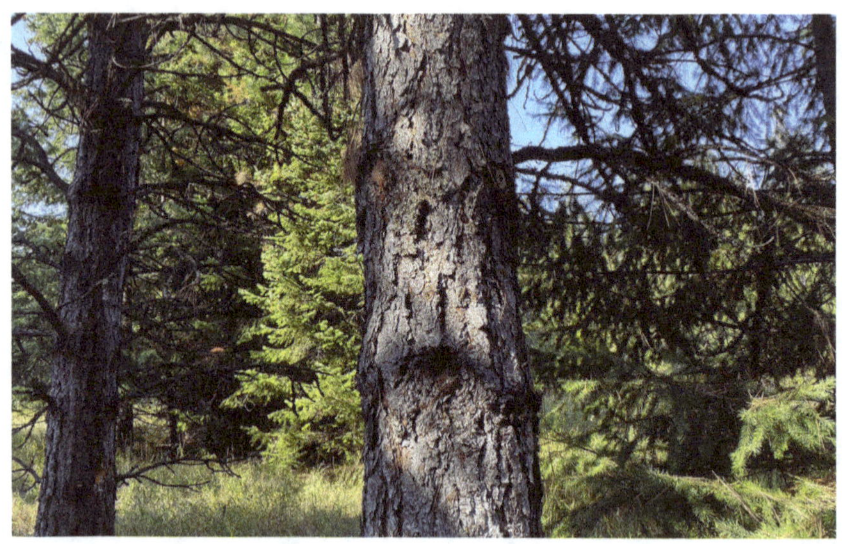

# Tree Punk

It's fair to say that on occasion, one must take certain artistic liberties to "fill in the blanks" – Remember, this is a book about "perception" and not about the quaint "artwork", I want to share what my mind is seeing. That's why this has what to me is a yellow-ish hairline. (*remember – color blind!*)

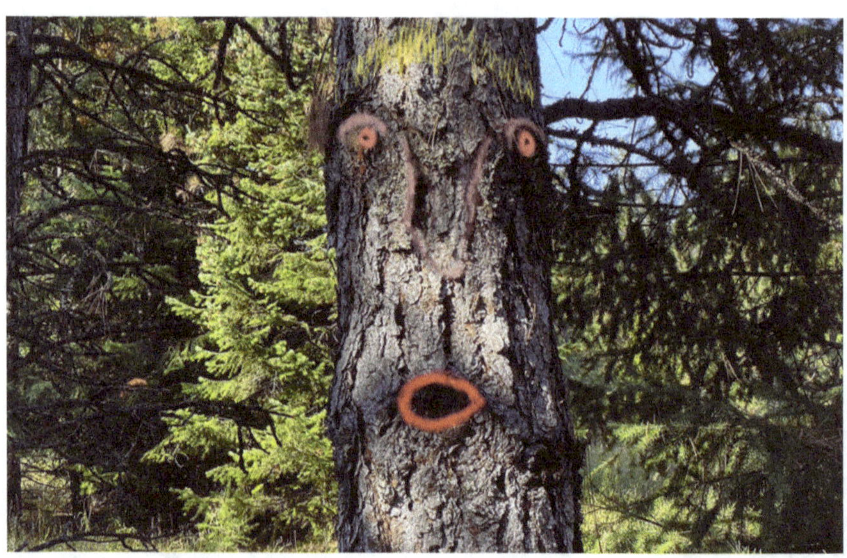

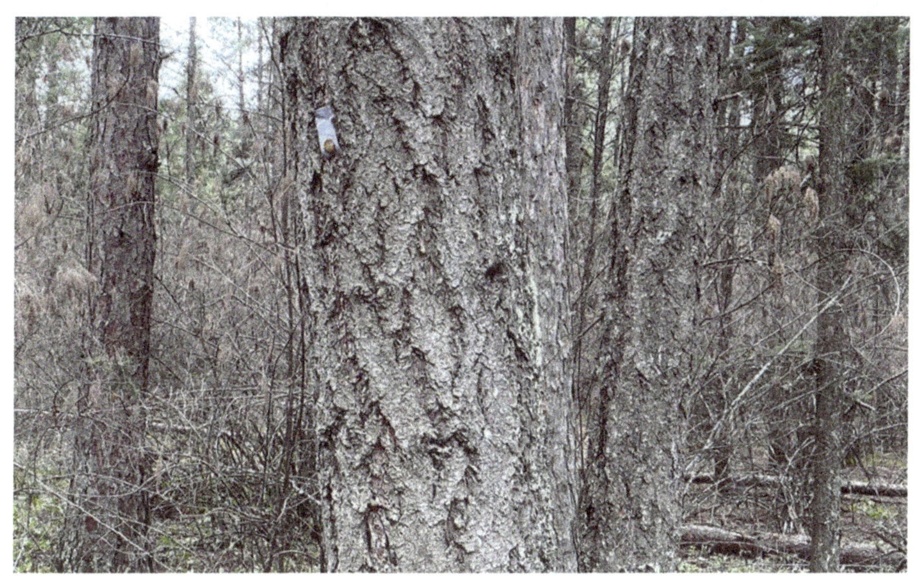

## Winky

Sometimes it's so obvious. Even simple, small marks on a tree can create the distinct look of a face. Almost no need to draw it. But, I did it anyway so you see what I saw! *(Hey, "see what I saw" -Remember the old "see-saws" – writing certainly has it's ups and downs, eh?)*

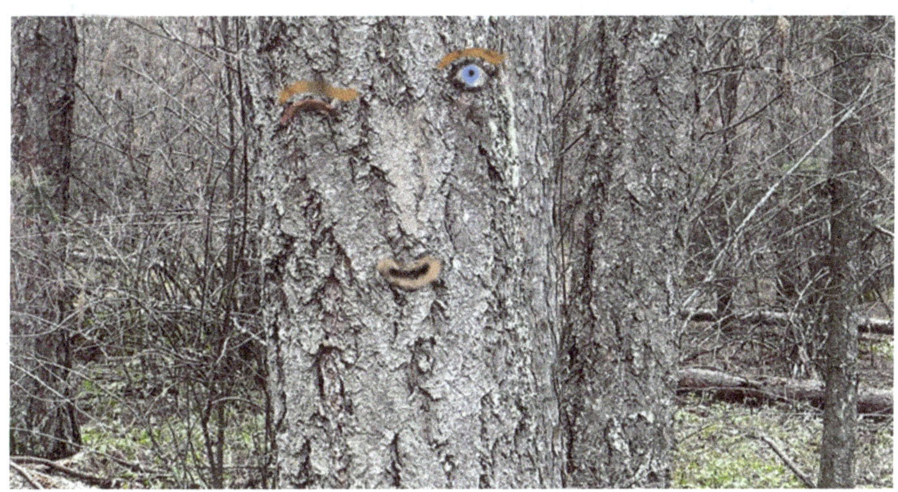

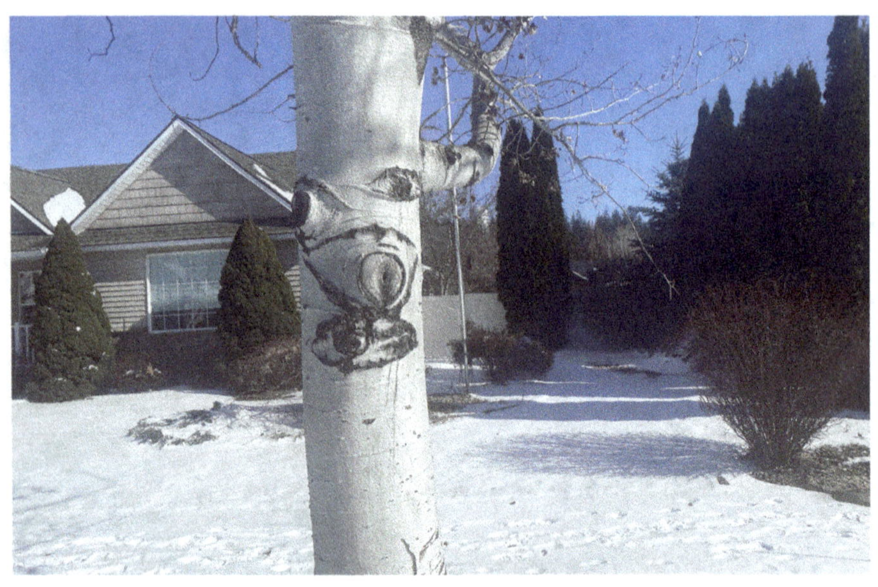

# Piggy

Maybe it's the nose but this has a distinctly piggy feel, don't you think? I can't get over how funny some of these trees look to me. The eyes and mouth are just what came out when I started adding some texture and color.

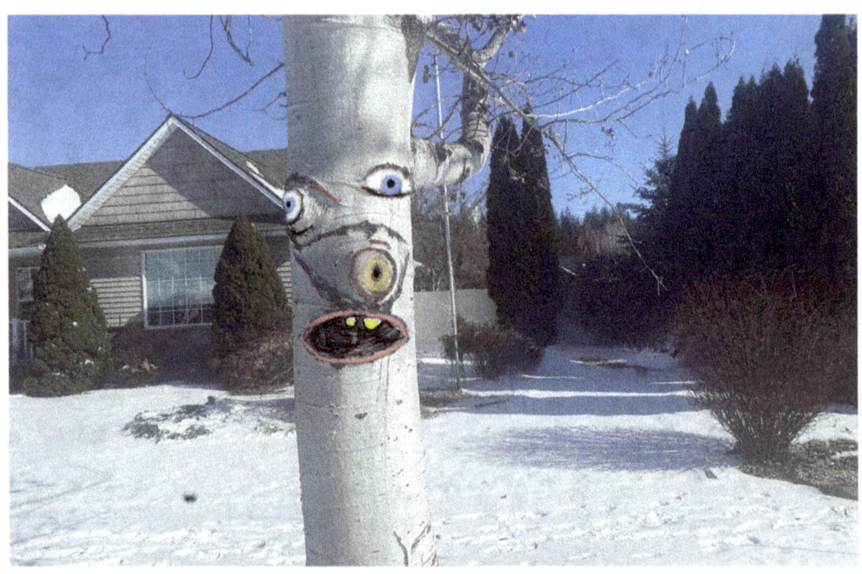

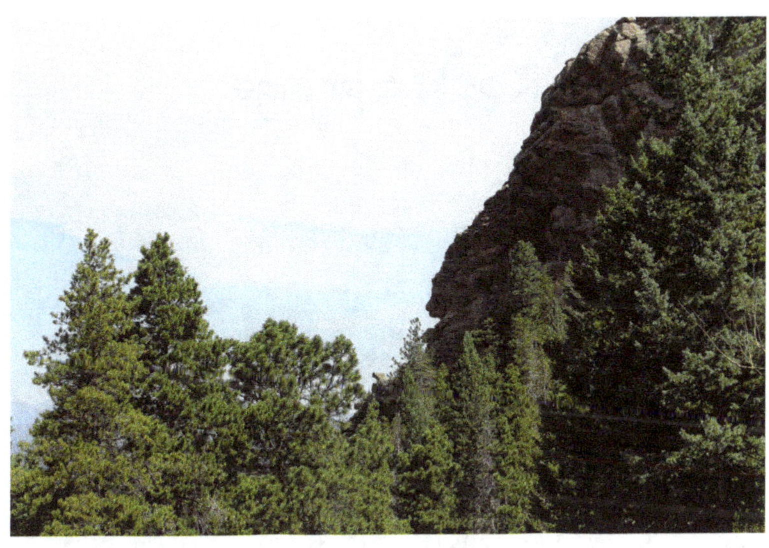

# Cliff Zen

Now we're in Colorado – this area is near WonderVu, CO on the way from Boulder to Nederland.

The "face" of the cliff seemed to be looking out as if to wonder about life itself…

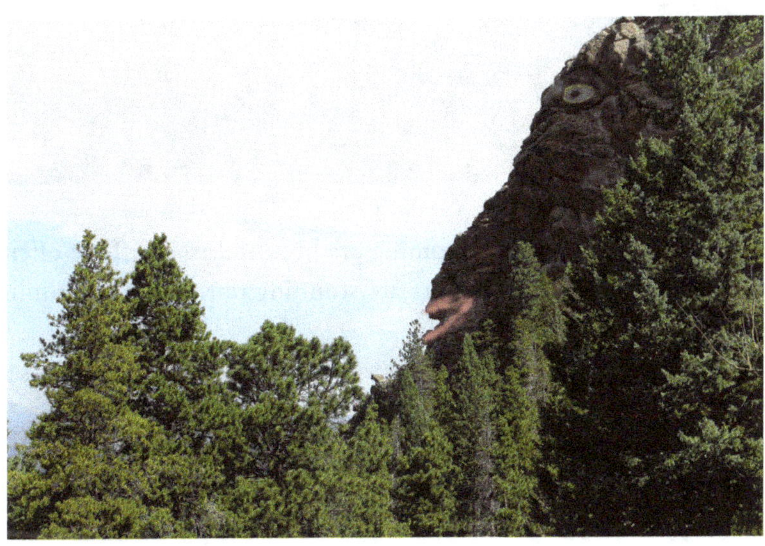

# Rock Springs

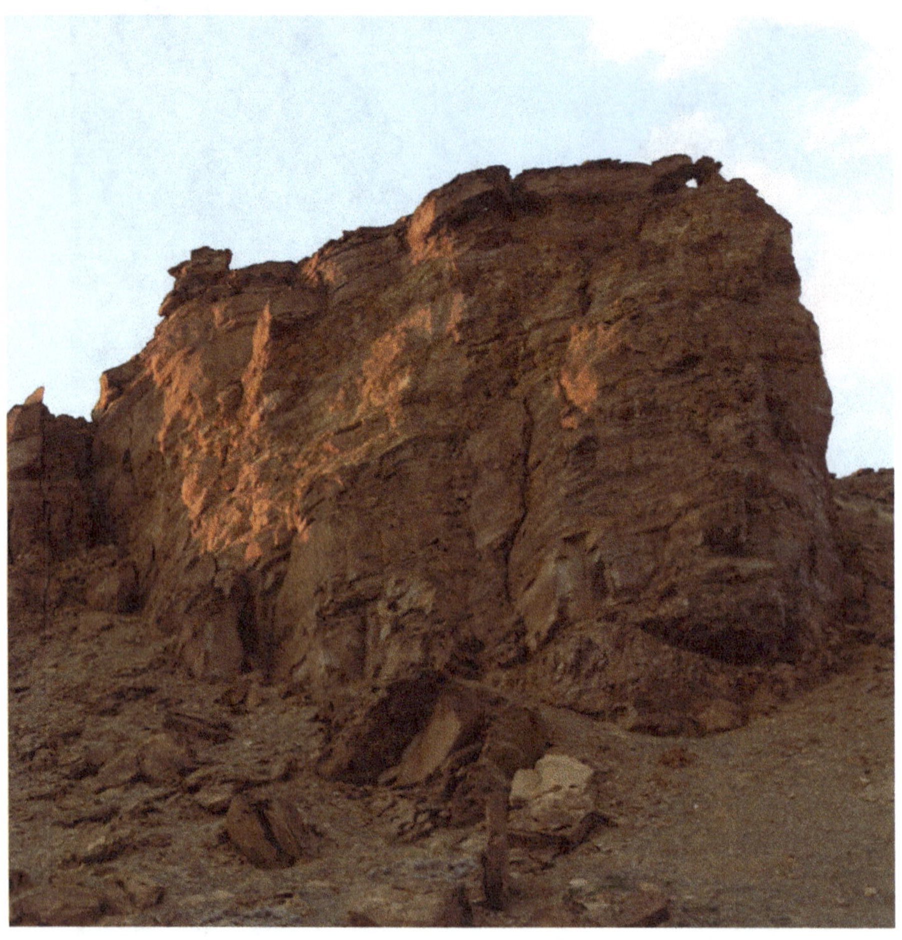

The hills in the south area of Wyoming are beautiful to see. They offer every shape and size and the warm colors are stunning during the last sunlight of the day.

This rock formation is near Rock Springs, Wyoming. The face was so obvious to me.

*Can you see it?*

# Mister Butte

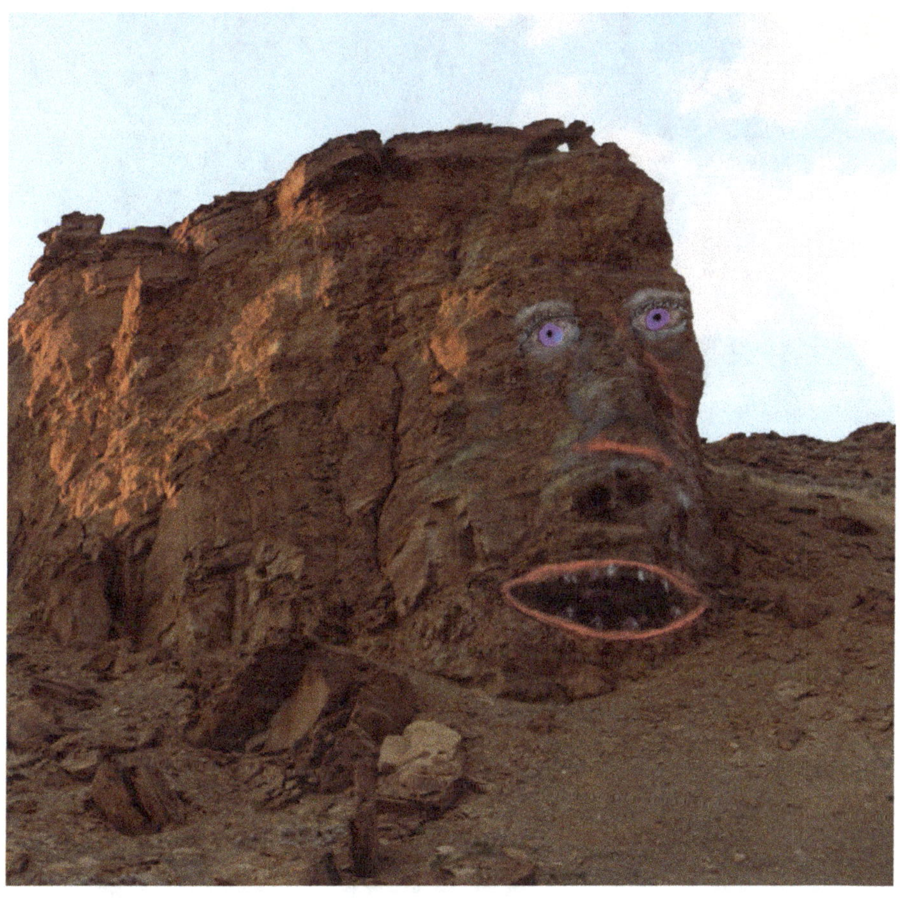

I really do marvel at how the images come to life. This was such a natural face on the end of that chunk of rock.

Southern Wyoming is really a wonderful place to visit and full of rock formations such as this one.

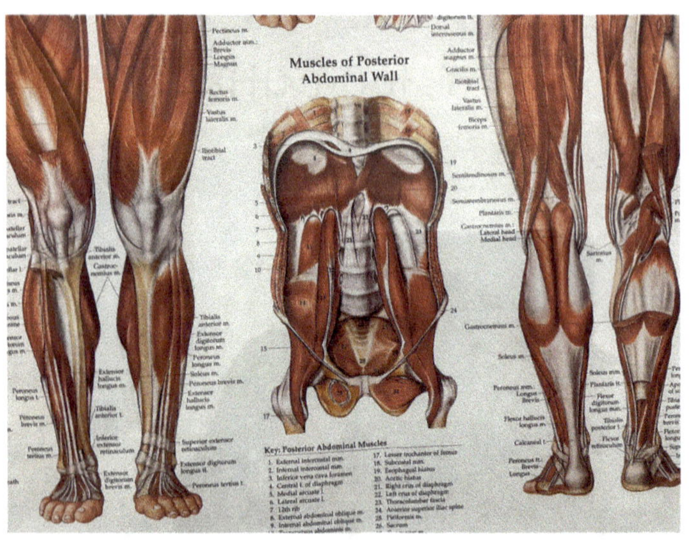


# The Crazy Alien

So… I was sitting in the waiting room at my doctor's office. On the wall I see this interesting poster.

And smack dab in the middle of the poster what appears?

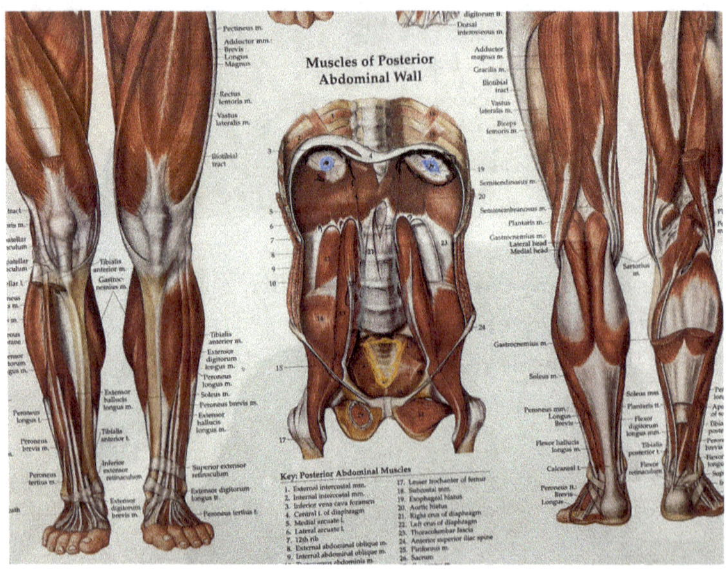

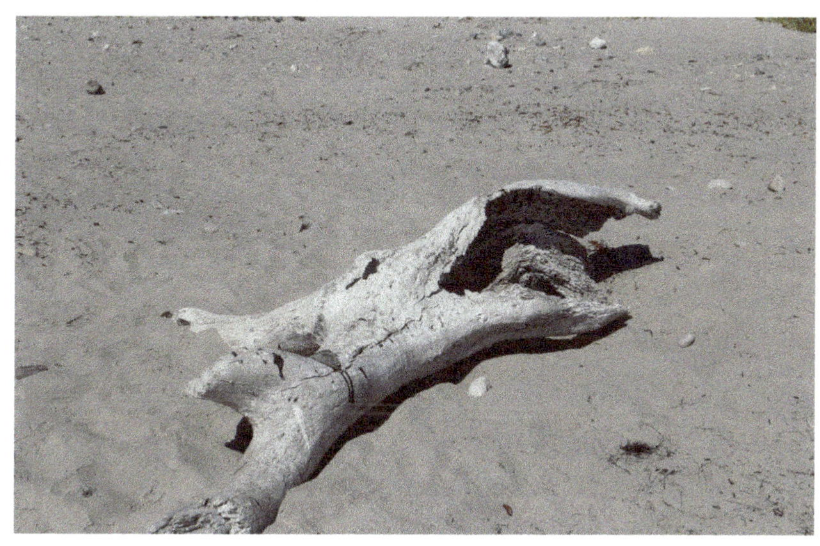

# Log Jaw

I saw this while walking on Jalama Beach. An old log?

Driftwood? Or maybe the remains of a creature with its mouth still open? To me, it looks like a creature with long jaws and the mouth is wide open – maybe a huge tongue in there.

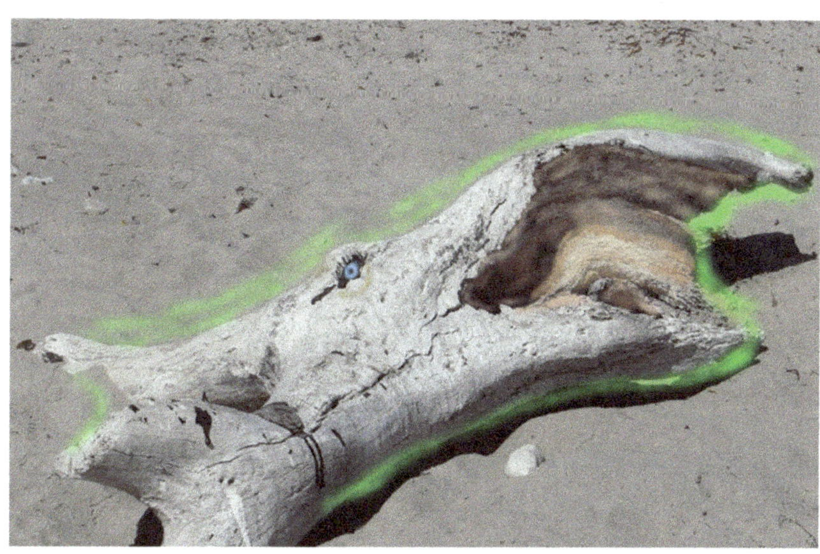

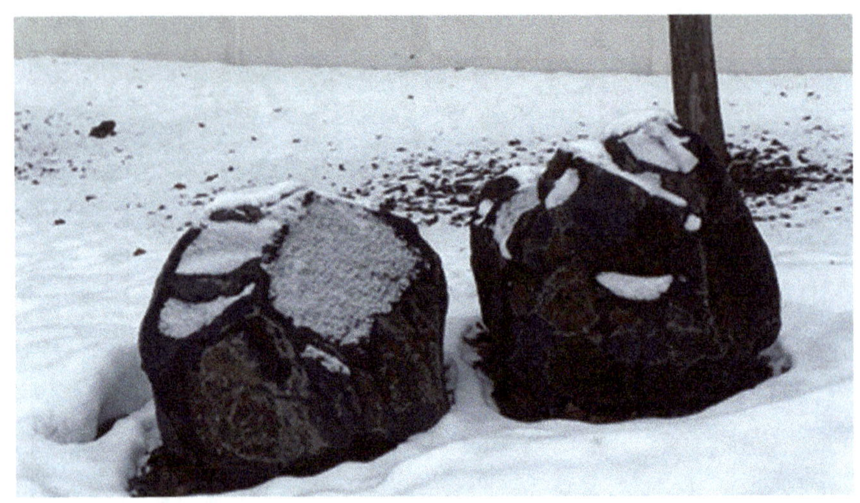

## Smirk Rock

This rock looks like it's up to no good. That smile leans more toward a smirk and that suggests some mischievous action going on… *hummm.*

*What do you think? This chap must have been naughty!*

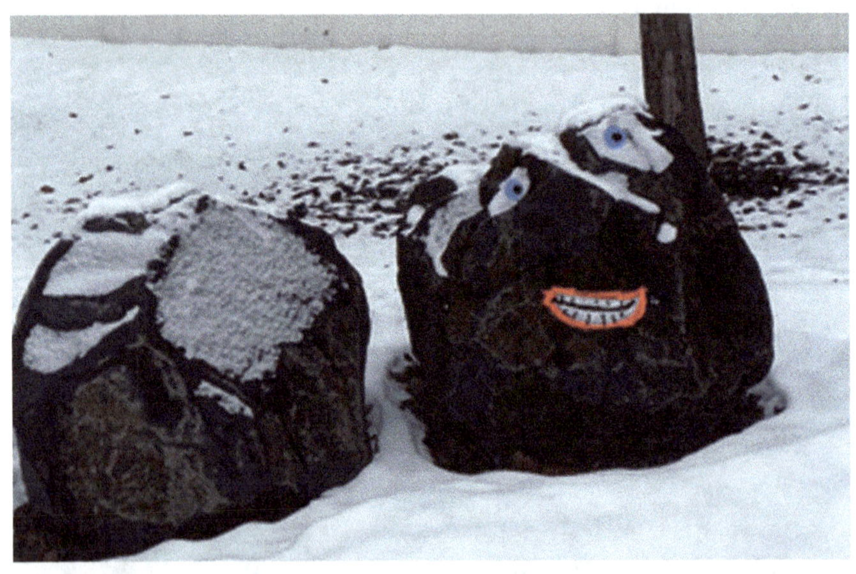

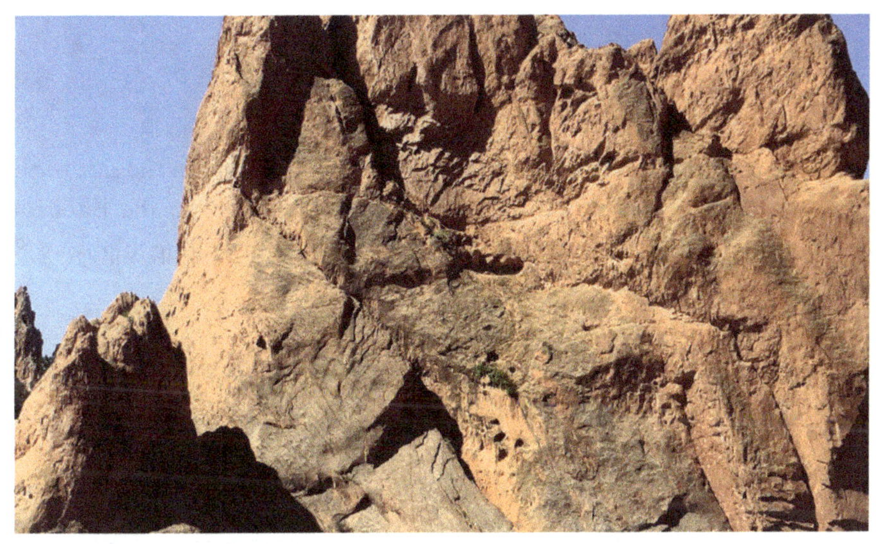

# Rocky

Garden of the Gods in Colorado Springs, CO. Rock climbers paradise, for sure. It is amazing to me that rock climbers take such a chance to climb a sheer rock wall. What the climbers do not realize! This creature is waiting for them to slip up and pop into that black hole :-)

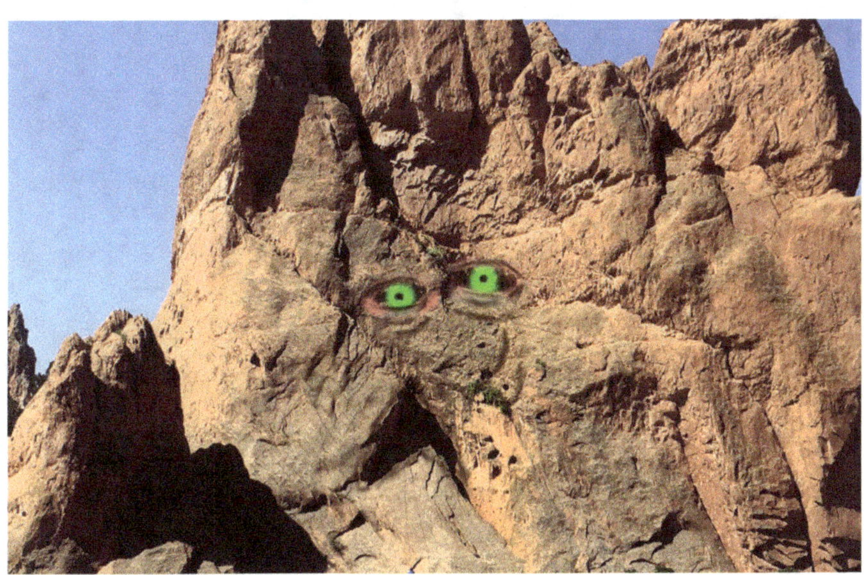

# The Challenge

Ok, here's the challenge... see how many faces you can find in the side of this mountain. I think this was in Montana near Lake Como in the Bitterroot Mountains. We like that entire valley when traveling along highway 93 through the Bitterroots.

They filmed the video series called, "Yellowstone" along this road and I agree with the Duttons, this is a beautiful and magical place well worth saving and keeping developers away from it.

*How many faces can you find?*

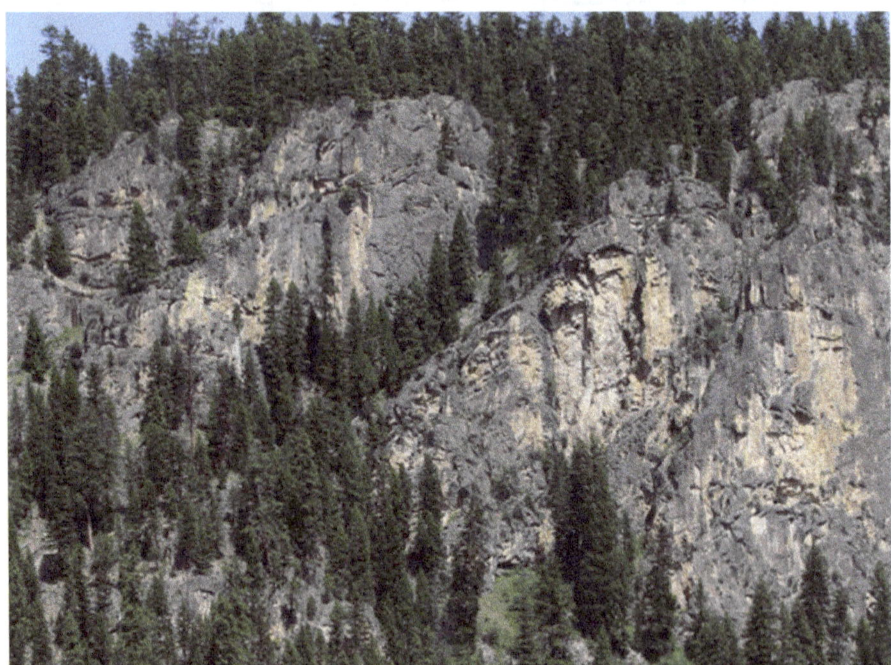

# Face Mountain

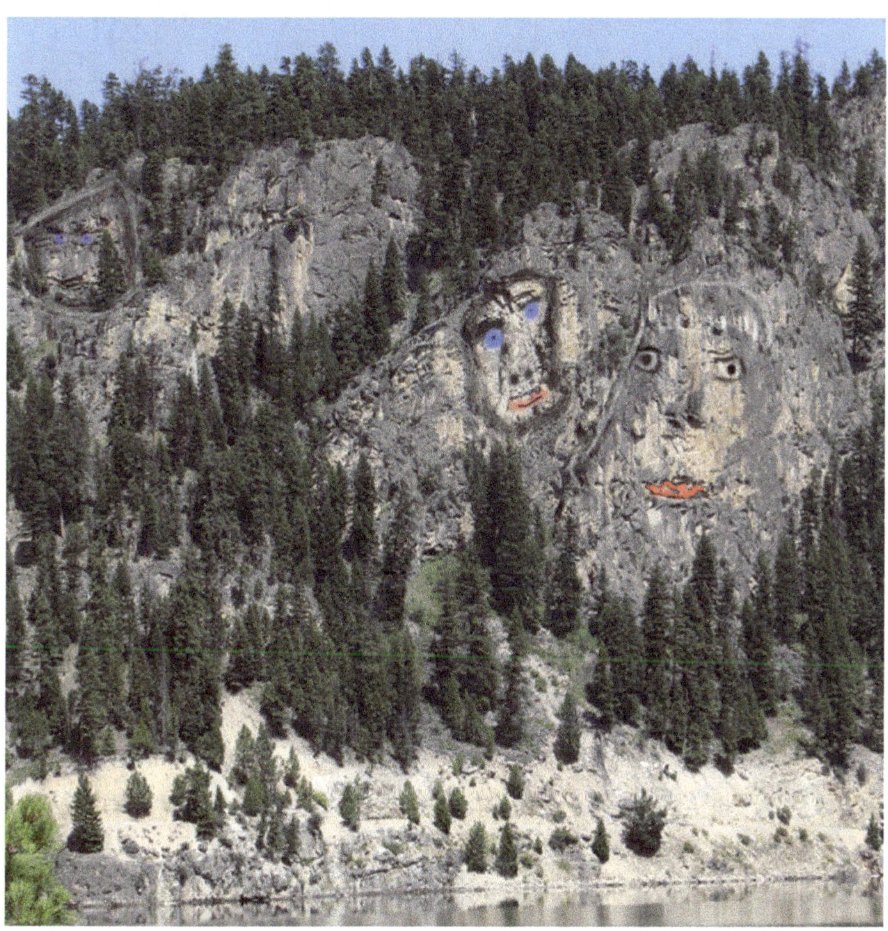

Did you find some faces? It's amazing how many times this happens. We (us humans) are just built and wired to see patterns of things that are important to our survival and recognizing a face seems to rule our brain.

I outlined a few that I saw but maybe there's more? Hope you find this as fascinating as I do!

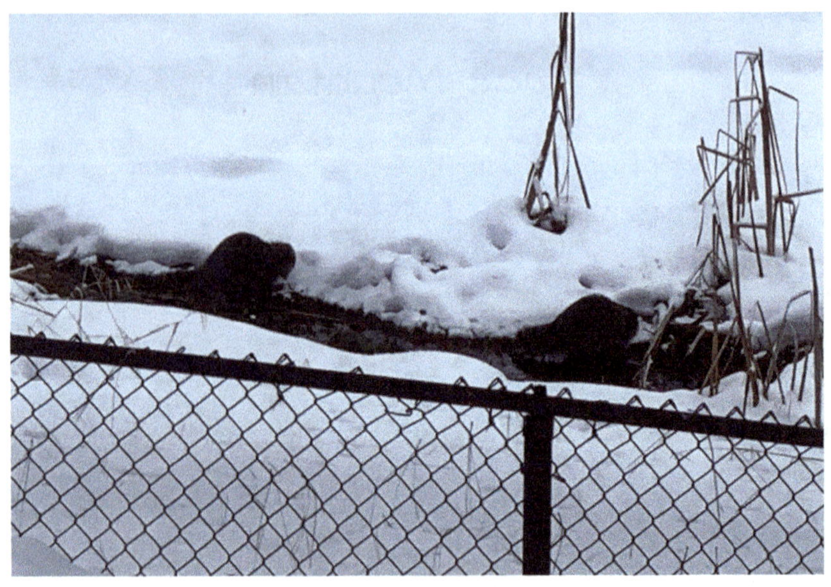

## Lab Creek

This creek often has wildlife looking for food. The exposure for the picture is pretty dark so I'll tell you these are two raccoons in the creek. But the dark profile told another story about two Labrador dogs that could not resist the water!

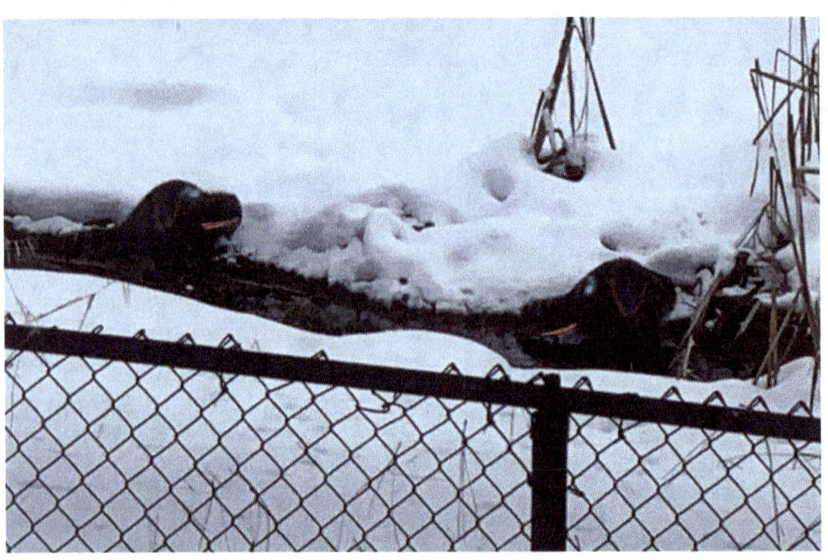

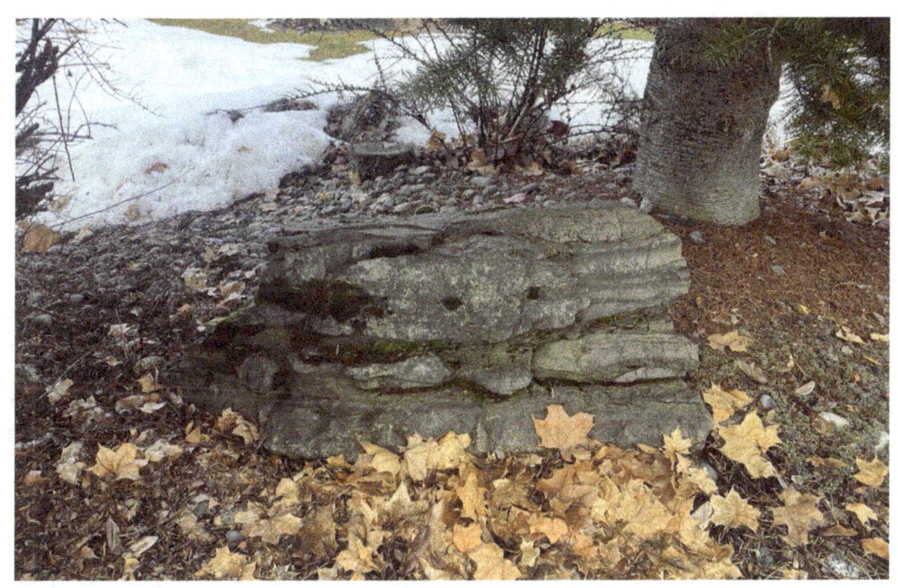

## Two Hole

I am so curious about those holes. What might have caused the two holes?

Whatever it was, it certainly formed a nice face outline.

Seems like a happy little rock…

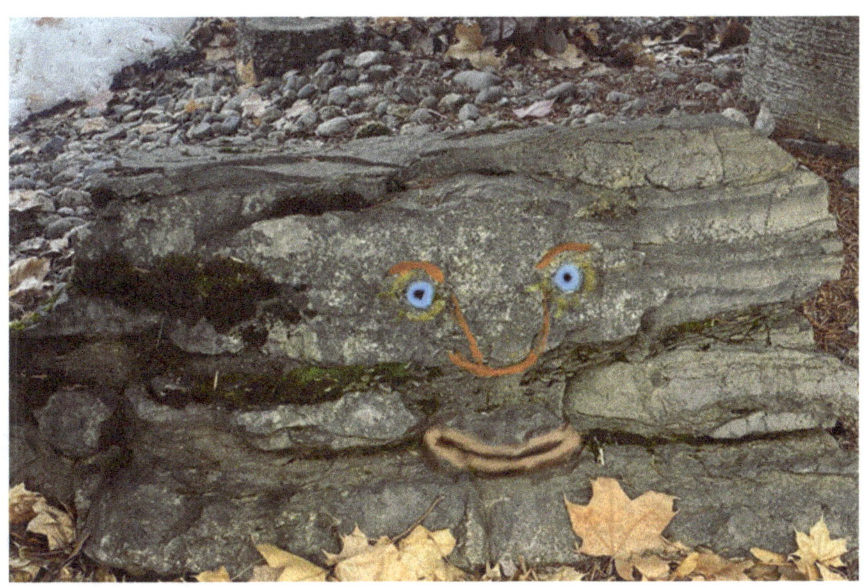

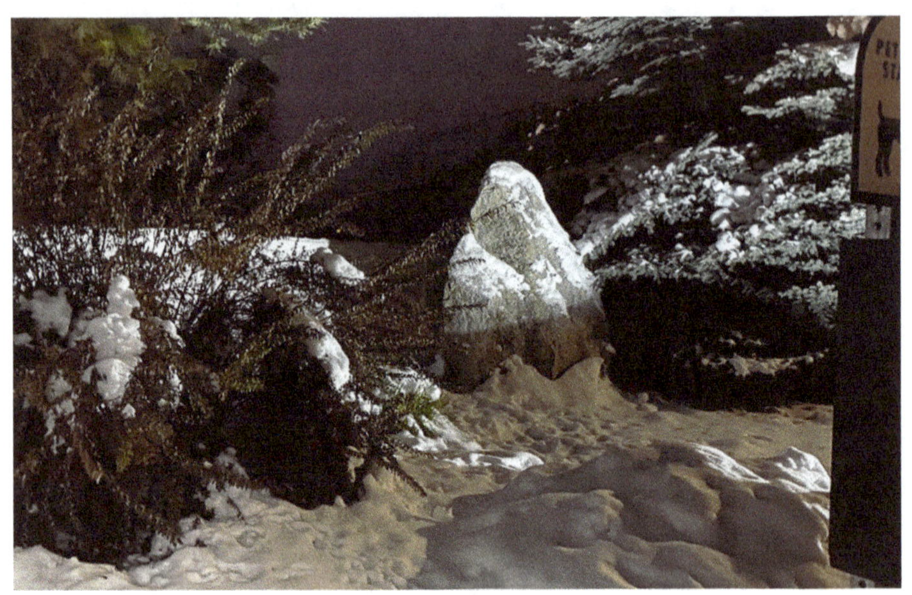

# Sasquatch

What? Yeti – Sasquatch – the abominable snowman! Right here in my neighborhood. When this images appear to me, it's so clear in my mind. Does that happen to you as well?

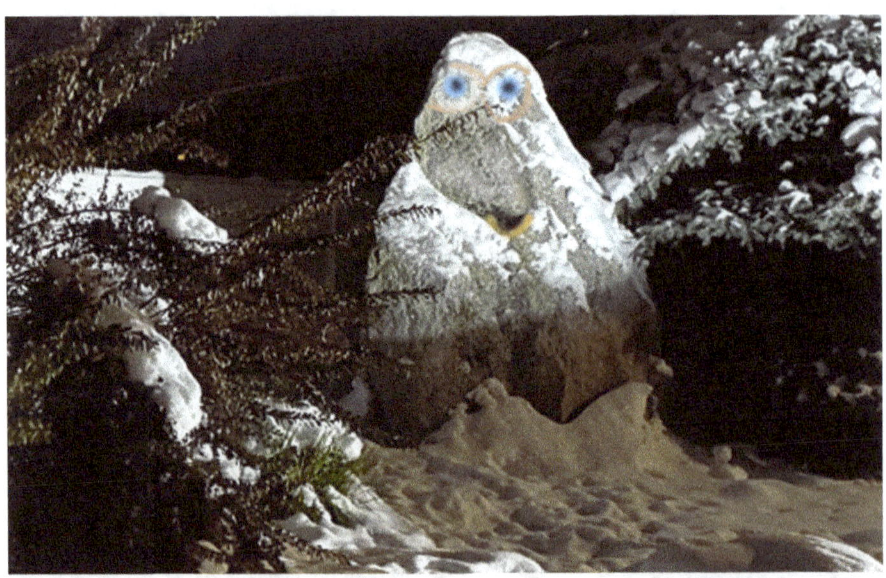

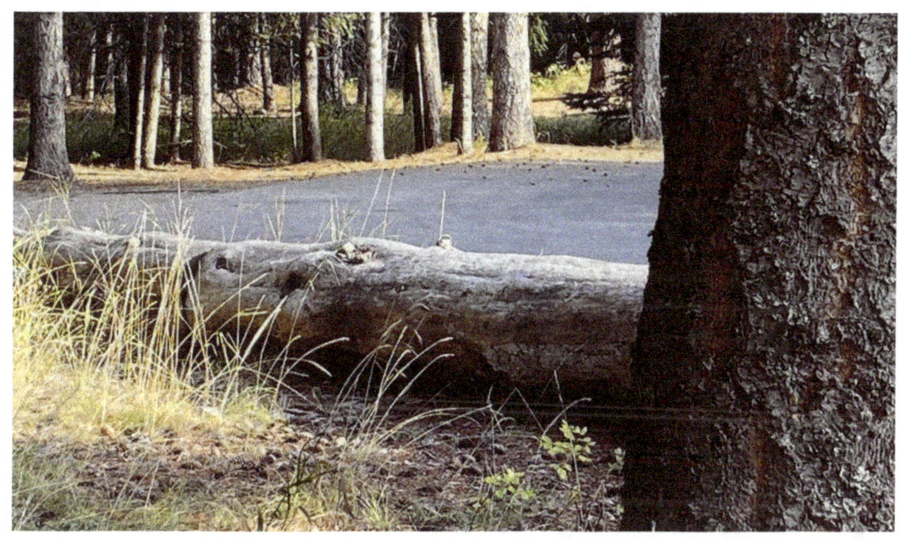

# Sneaky Log

After taking this picture, I wondered why I did it. This picture took a bit of searching to understand what I had seen – Then it appeared! Look down at the tops of the grass. Given the expression, it appears the creature was just as surprised as I was when I found it!

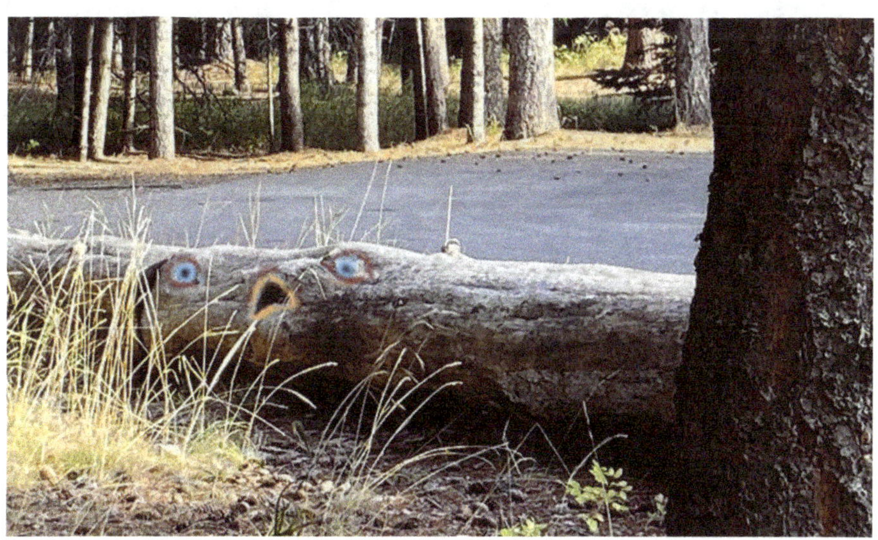

# Forest Horse?

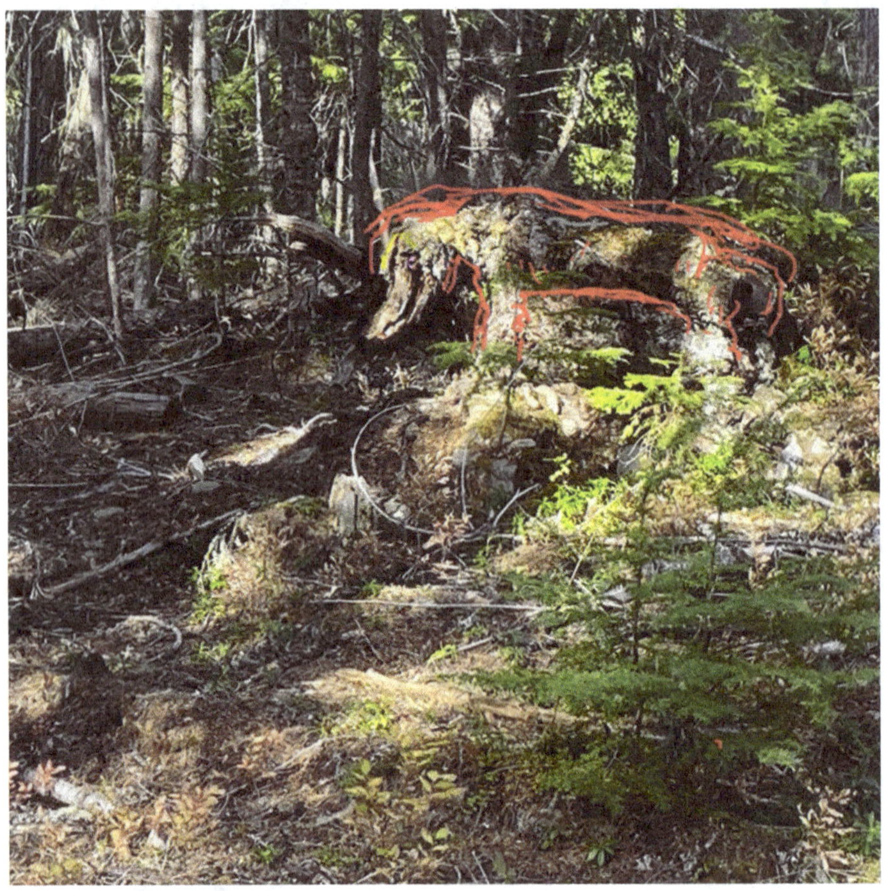

I'm pretty sure we were hiking around the trails in Priest Lake State Park in North Idaho. This old log reminded me of a horse when I first saw it. Then that nose came fully into view and that made me think about a duck-billed platypus – now I'm completely confused but it's still a fun thing to think about.

# Horse-icorn or Uni-horse

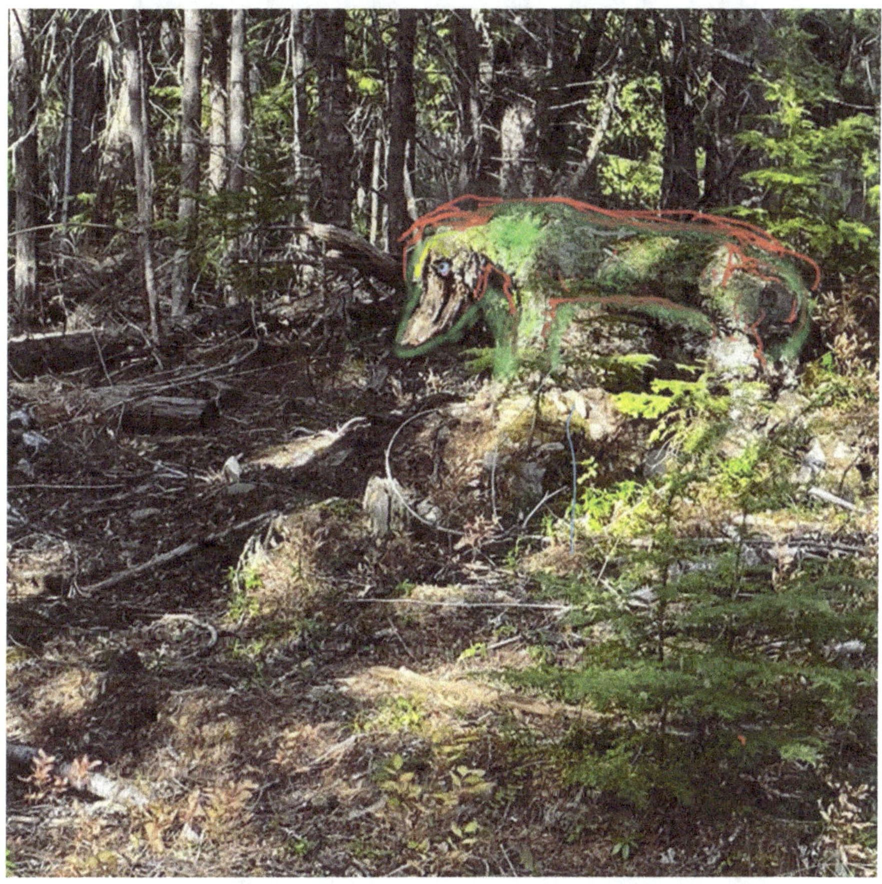

Certainly not a complete unicorn – So we have no idea what this is. It could be a combination of a duck-billed platypus, a horse and a unicorn.

Or maybe just a log with moss... either way it's a fun and magical image of a "thing" sitting in the woods. I think this is on the trail along the creek at Priest Lake Campground in North Idaho.

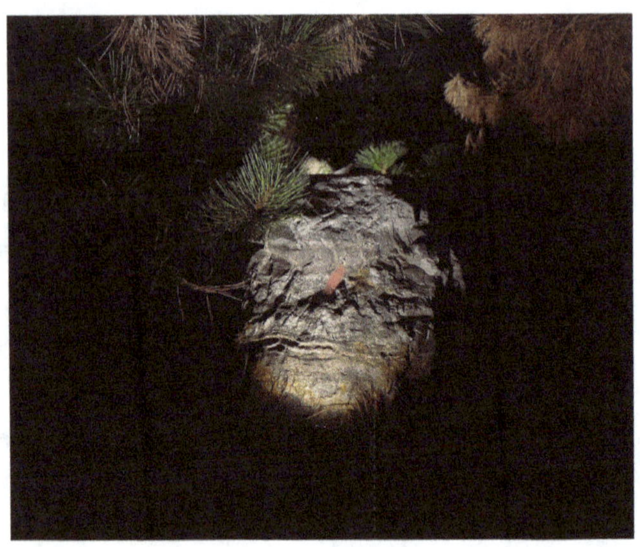

# Ape Rock

This rock has to have some DNA from a primate or some human connection – even without the additional artwork, this is just too "person-looking" – it never fails to amaze me how many *things* look like a creature.

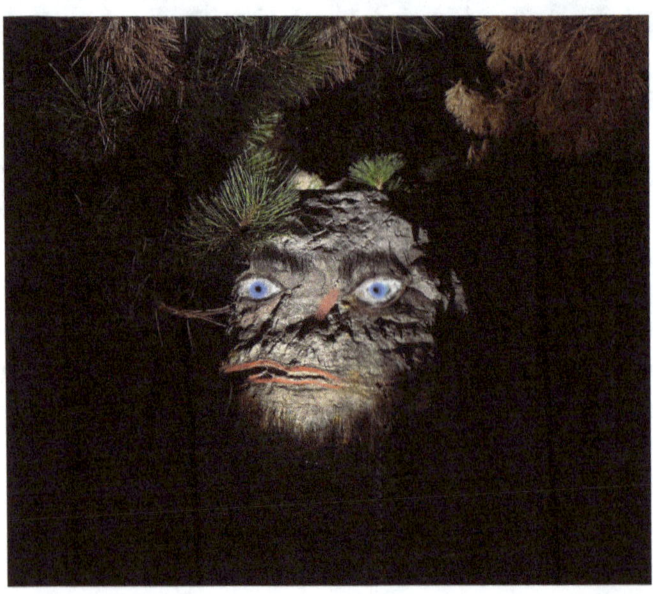

# Artwork versus Perceptions

I need to explain about the artwork. If you can actually call my drawings "art." – It should be painfully obvious to you by now that I am not an artist.

Many of the females in my family have been real artists but I did not acquire that talent. I do write music, but drawing… not so much. *(find my music by searching iTunes or Amazon music using my last name in the search box: "Eittreim")*

What I have attempted to show in this book are the *perceptions of things* that I see beyond the object itself. That desire to convey "perceptions", required some ability with drawing tools but admittedly, I have not improved my drawing skills much beyond grammar school.

This was a hard decision at first – I wanted the drawings to be very nice but at the same time, I want to make sure the drawings represent what I see in my brain. That meant I would have to have a well defined ability to explain to an artist just what my mind is seeing, or I would have to try and draw the image myself. I guess it's obvious which way that decision went.

So, bear with me on this one – the art is whimsical, for sure. But it does more accurately capture what I see – so maybe it's ok. The important thing to remember is that I want to share the perceptions and this is the only way I can think of how to do that. By personally taking on the drawing tasks, I am able to reflect a truer picture of what I see. And yes, many times it is pretty whimsical. If you look at the original images *(usually, the image on the top of each page is unedited)* – look deeply at the original and see what comes to your mind. Then look at the bottom image where I have added some color, eyes and other features.

Do you see the same image? Does the image you see have the same expression or "feeling?" Looking deeper into the object I get a sense of "feel" – hard to explain that feeling but I hope you are understanding what I mean. It does add some interesting dimensions to everyday life.

*Maybe we are not as "alone" as we think?*

# One Big Old Rock

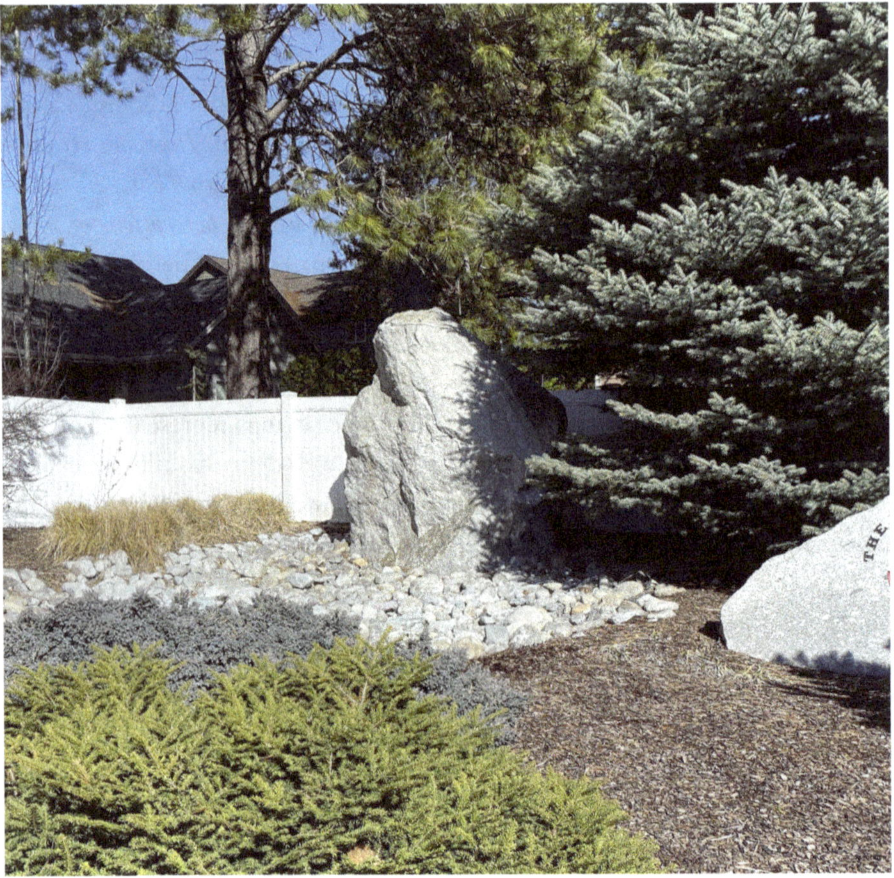


Ok, tell me you see this face profile. You HAVE to see this one – the eye, nose and a sort of puckered lip. Even the cheek with the slight shadowing.

This rock has been sitting in the back of this landscaping area for about 8 years. I have walked past here many times and never noticed.

*Until today!*

# So Stoned

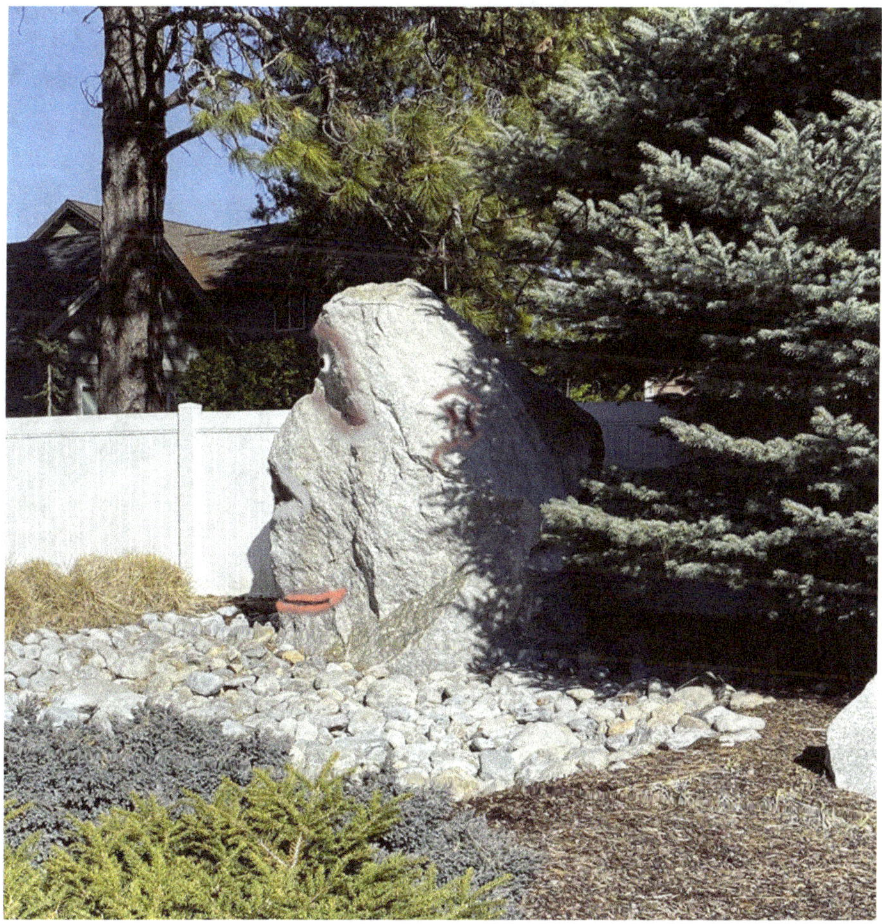

I have walked past this rock for almost 8 years and never stopped to say hello. Until a few days ago – Elizabeth and I were walking our dog, Ellie Grace.

When I stopped for a moment to tie my shoe, I looked around and to my astonishment, this chap was just patiently waiting.

*Sometimes, I am amazed at how blind I am to the world around me.*

# The Old Stump

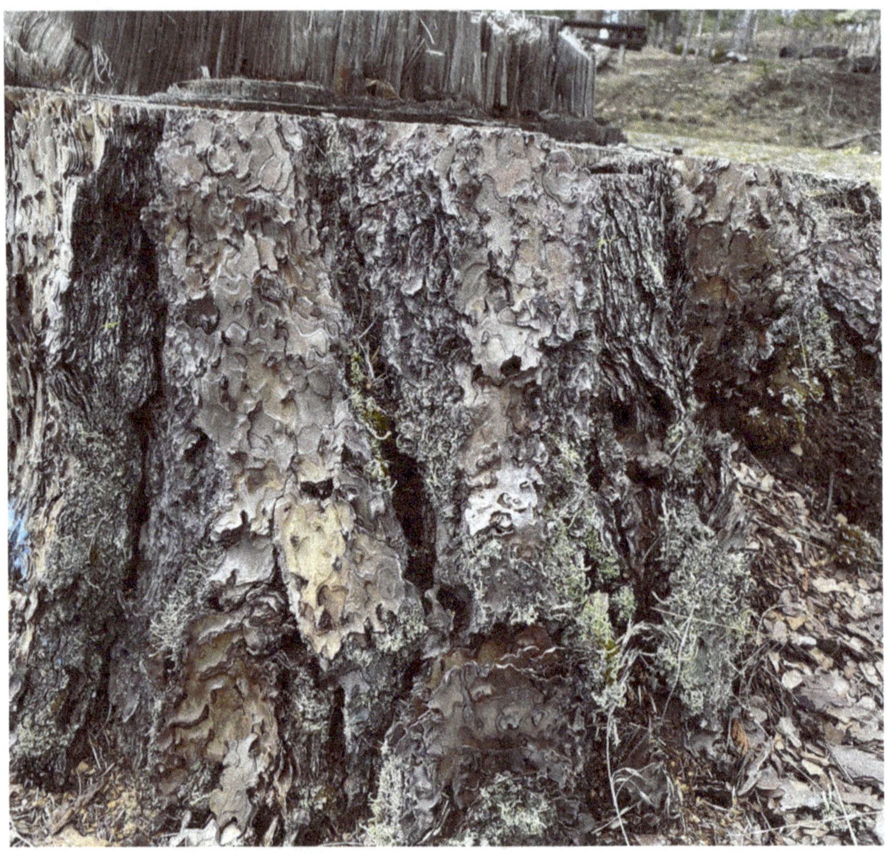

This location is in the Sam Owen Campground near Hope, Idaho.

The area is a deer preserve and has been a favorite location for us over the past 40 years. We have camped here with our kids, and 3 different sets of chocolate labs. Have I ever seen this tree before? Nope. Not in the past 40 years of walking past this tree have I stopped to notice.

And now? I see at least 3 distinct faces in what is left of this marvelous tree.

# Totally Stumped

To me, this is reminiscent of an old noble Indian. This area was home to the Kalispels Indian tribe and perhaps, some spirits. I certainly feel a love and respect for this land and I hope I'm as kind to the land as they were over the years. Sam Owen Campground has a special place in my heart and I'm sure for many other people.

A fun fact: *The small town of Hope is nearby, as is "Beyond Hope" and a 3rd community – you guessed it – "Above Beyond Hope!"*

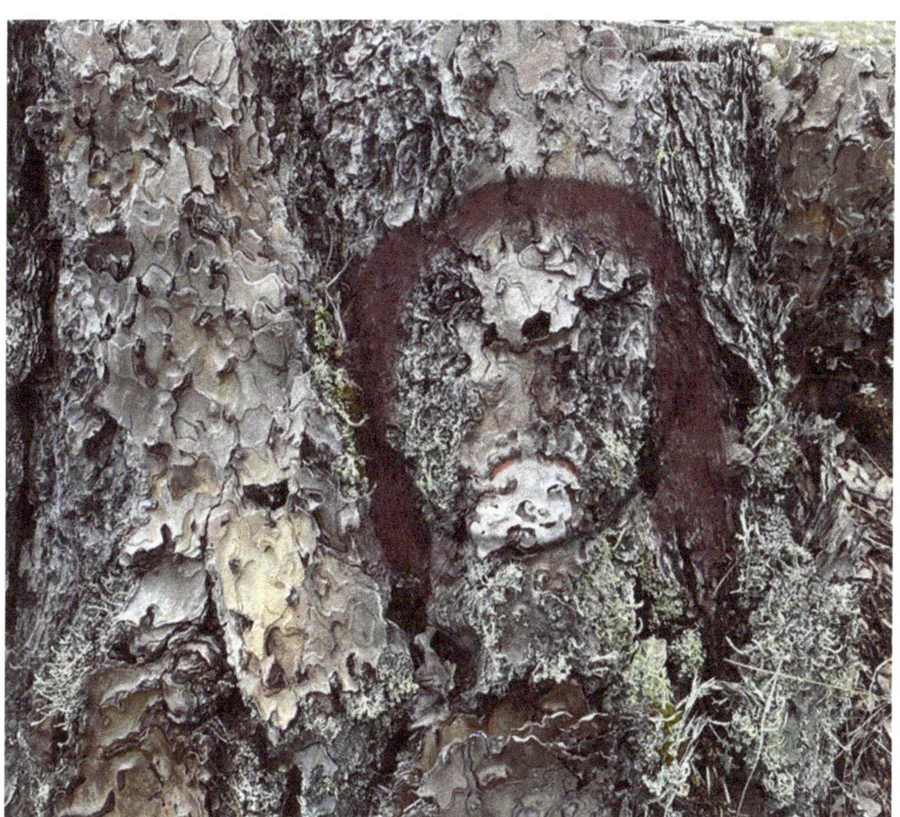

# Monkey Face

Did you know that Ponderosa Pines bark gives a smell like vanilla when warm? The bark on old trees is absolutely beautiful. So many designs in the cracks and crevices. And now this one? I see at least 3 distinct faces in what is left of this marvelous tree. Looking at a bit of a slant, I see another face of an angry monkey.

*This one is sort of a goofy monkey face.*

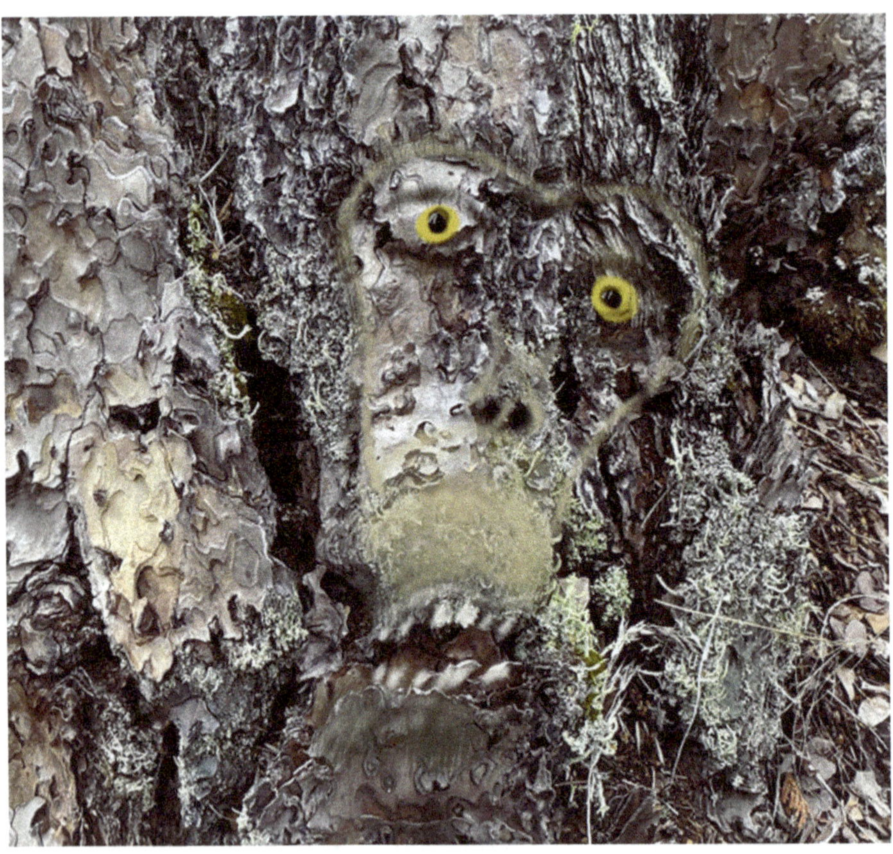

# The Other Side

So, have a look at the other side of the monkey stump… this was certainly a large old tree that they had to remove because of some rot problems that were prevalent around the Sam Owen Campground. As we walked up to this stump, I saw a couple of faces.

*Then when we walked past, yet another face on the other side!*

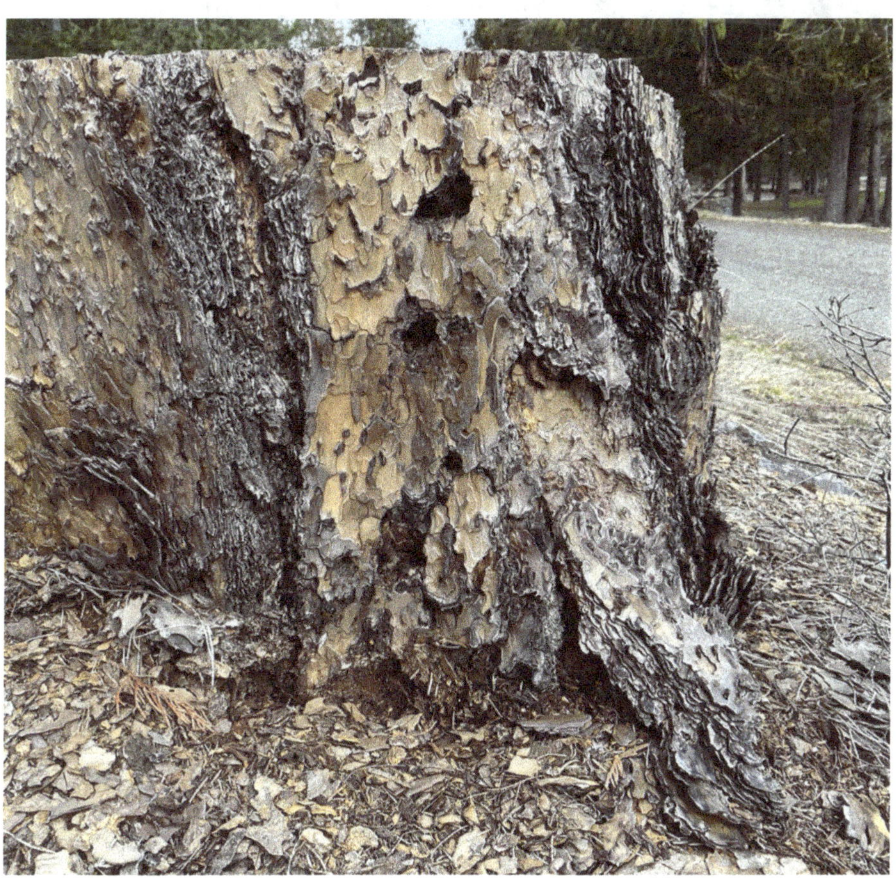

# The Old Man

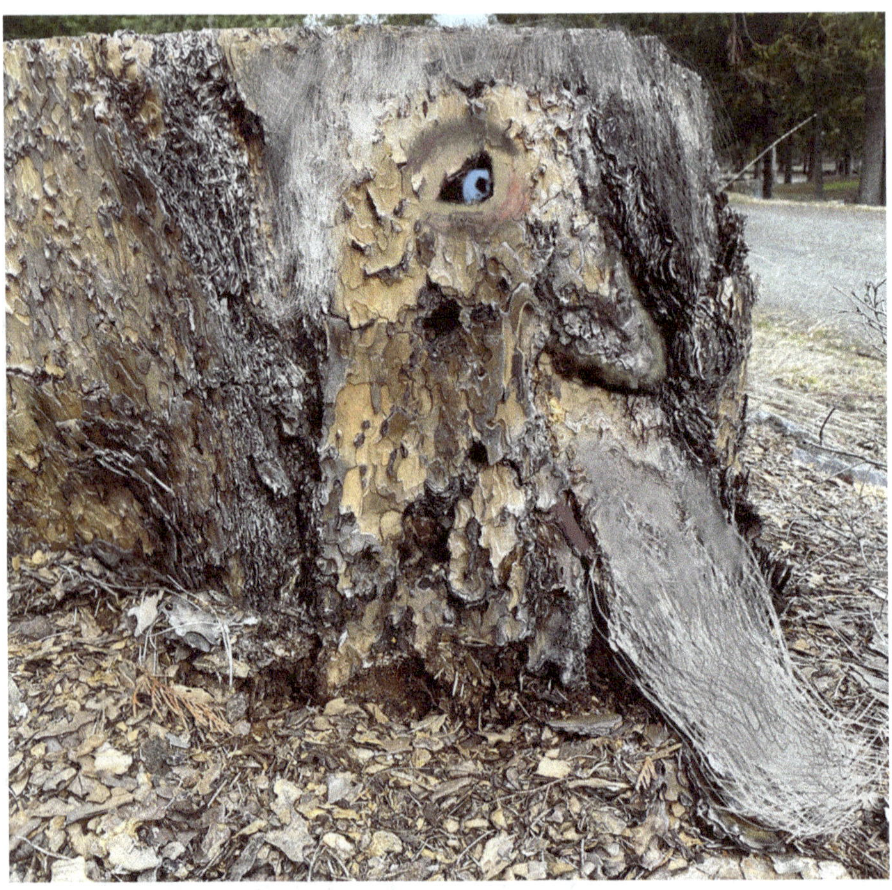

This is the same stump with monkey face. This side has an old man face that has a very long, grey beard.

This is the other side of the monkey face stump. I was pretty amazed at seeing several faces in a single stump.

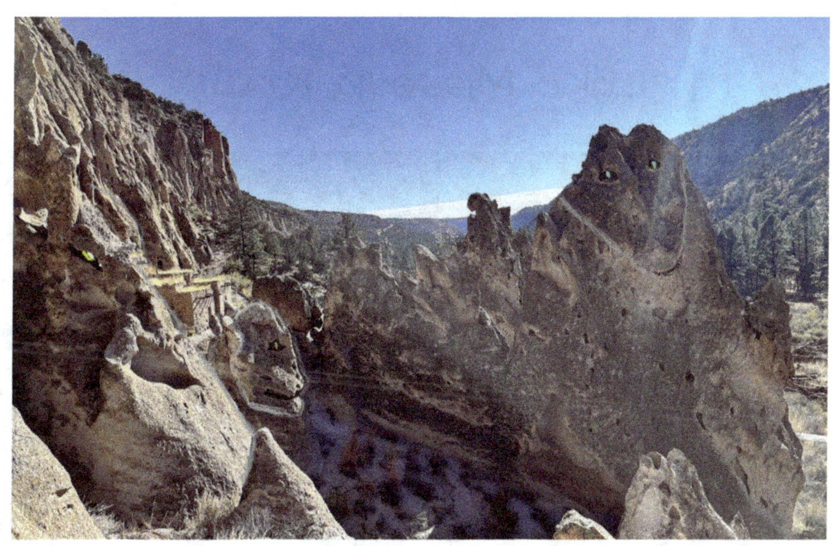

## Dino Mountain

The American Southwest – what a great area to see dinosaurs in the landscape. This image was taken by a friend (used by permission – thanks, Kim) that shared my sense of seeing "things" in the rocks. Maybe the spirit of the old dinosaurs lives on and we only have to look around us and let our imagination come to life.

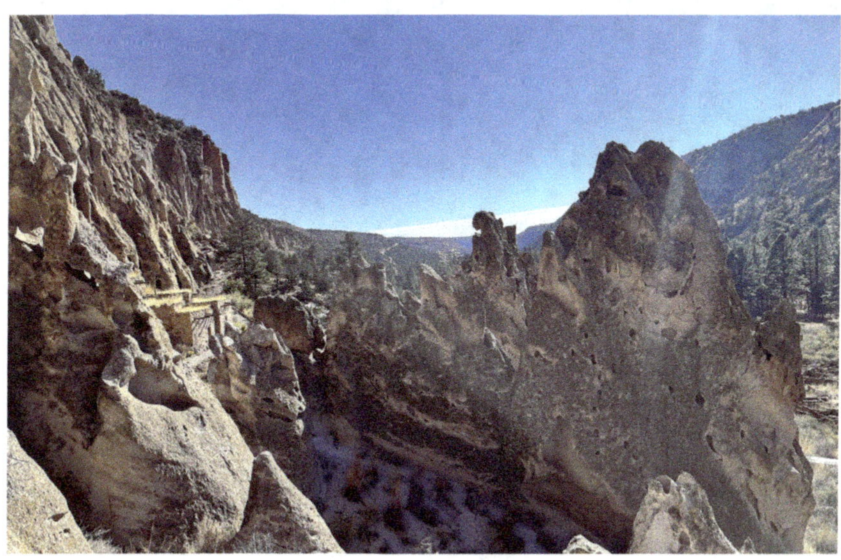

# Lake Missoula Rock

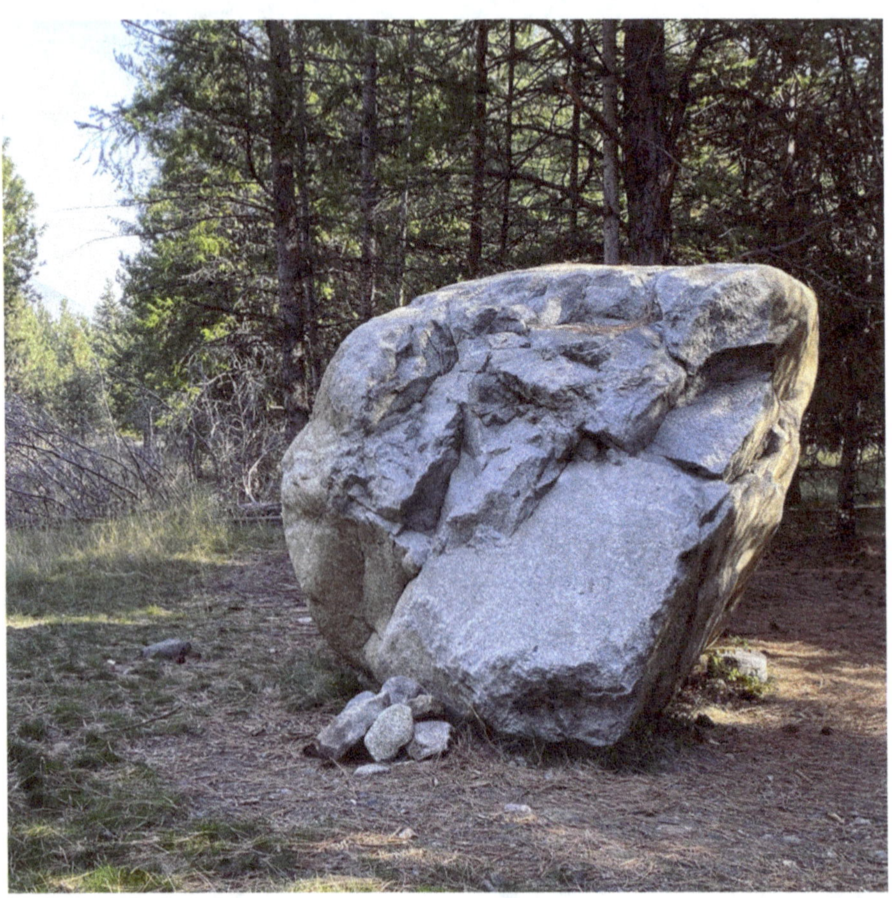

An ancient flood from Lake Missoula happened about 12,000 years ago – that flood deposited huge car sized boulders across Idaho, Washington and Oregon.

During a walk in Farragut State Park, I happened to see one of those ancient rocks. Maybe it still has a few thoughts about the floating icebergs full of boulders as they rode the flood all the way from Montana? Who knows what the creature is looking at. Or is it just an odd shape?

*What do you see?*

# Rock & Roll

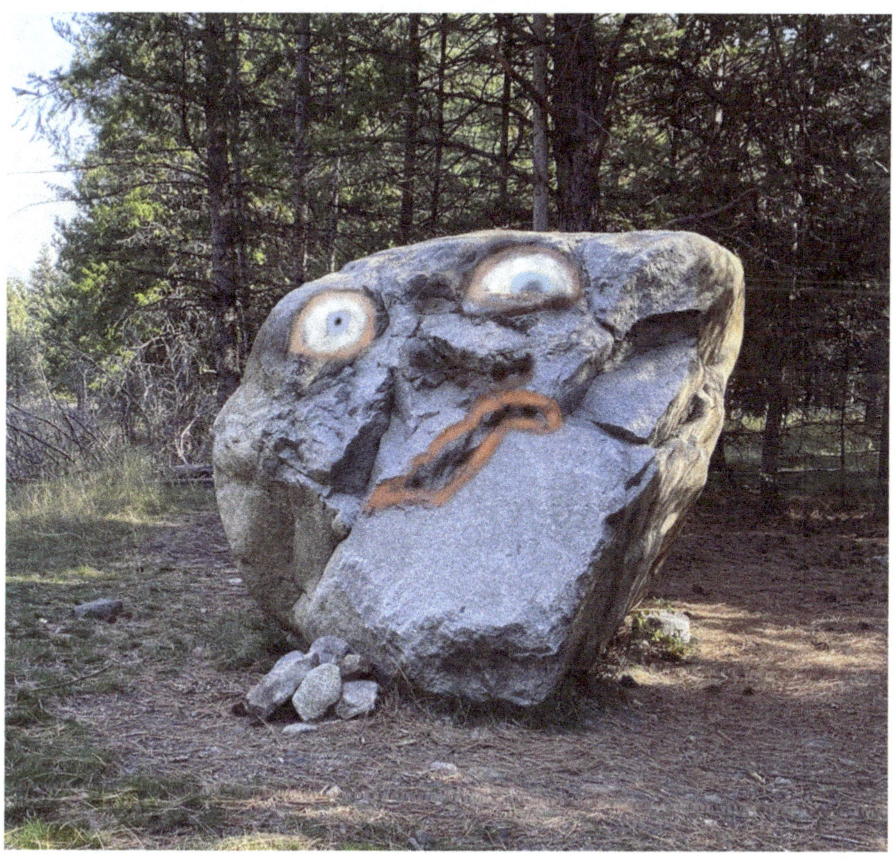

So, walking around the woods, what do you see and feel. Have you ever had that "*feeling*" that someone or "*something*" is looking at you? Have you been alone in the forest and "felt" a presence?

This rock is a good example of what happens when I'm hiking. Many times I have glanced around and I see things like this! So, what do you think? Can you see it?

*Do you see the face looking at you with those wild eyes?*

# The Curling Beard

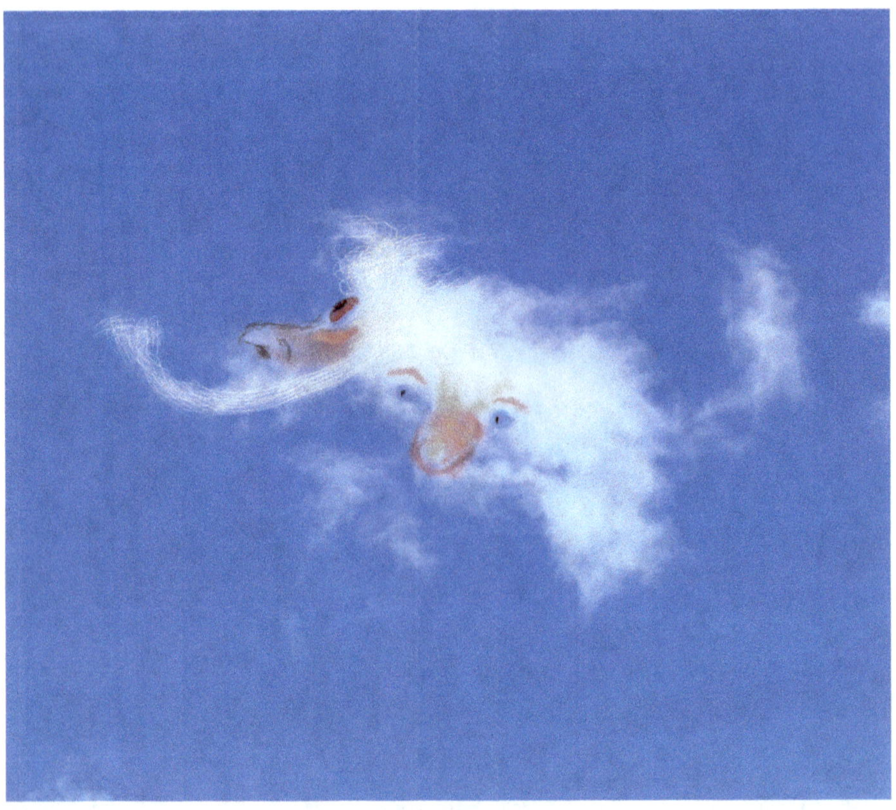

By the way, remember the very first image in the beginning of this book? That image of the cloud? Right at the beginning of "*I See Things*", we offered this image and suggested what I see in the cloud.

When I asked if you could see the old man with a curling beard and that other creature looking down, did you see this?

*Well, this is what I saw!*

# Color Blindness

*Oh, did I mention that I have a problem seeing colors?*

And yes, this is another interesting topic (other than my drawing ability) – I have a red-green color problem. Many items that I hear are really brown or tan – to me, these items are shades of green. Peanut butter? Some people? Many times I ask my wife about a color because I see two or more colors in the object but I can't come up with a name for that specific color. Often, my "colors that make that color" are correct but the end result is confusing to me and I struggle to find a name. Very odd defect in my vision system.

So, why do I mention color blindness? Because I am the one creating this whimsical "artwork." And some of the creatures that you see might be colorized in odd ways. But to me, that's what I see. Even in my "minds eye." Look at it this way – not only do you get to read a fun book, you get a lesson on what color blind people see! How cool is that?

So this might be a book about how objects change into other objects but in addition, you get to have a glimpse into the world of us humans that have color shifted vision problems.

When I was in grammar school, it was a very small country school. We had 8 kids in our class, 3 grades in one room with a single teacher. And yes, we did behave and we did learn quite well. But the point is that the school was very small and it was in the 1950's and the discovery of how to work with color blindness was not a topic we knew about.

From what I heard later is that the teachers told my parents that I was a little weird and they should have someone take a look at me. I apparently colored cows with green crayons. Well, that's because they look like that color to me!

*Nothing weird about it!*

# More About the Color Problems

Males have a 1 in 12 chance of being color blind. I am that lucky one in 12 so again, if you find some of the color choices in the "artwork" look a bit odd, please enjoy the experience of seeing how a color blind person sees and imagines life.

Color blindness is a pretty fascinating topic and several types and degrees of color blindness impact us in different ways. In the military, color blind soldiers seem to offer an advantage in certain situations:

---

THE chief characteristic which distinguishes colourblind people from those with normal vision, is a reduced ability to distinguish colours that are normally quite distinct.

Superficially, therefore, it would seem highly improbable that colour-blind persons could detect a camouflaged building that an ordinary observer would miss. This suggestion, however, which has come from the United States recently, is not wholly without foundation, as there are at least three ways in which certain colour-blind observers might see more than the ordinary person. For example, in a building camouflaged with large irregular patches of colour, the actual outline of the building may be lost in the jumble of these patterns. But the colour-blind person may be scarcely conscious of the variegated colours, so that to him the outline of the building may be almost unaffected by the camouflage. In the Ishihara test for colourblindness, certain of the cards actually use this principle; a faint blue figure is printed on a background of highly coloured dots of various hues. To the normal observer the blue figure is lost against the background, but the colour-blind person may spot it. Again, in the protanopic and protanomalous type of defect, reds and yellows appear darker than usual, and with certain colouring of building and background this could lead to an enhanced contrast and so give the colour-blind person his advantage.[1]

---

1 Colour-Blindness and Camouflage. *Nature* **146**, 226 (1940). https://doi.org/10.1038/146226a0

Note: The above paragraph is sourced from the U.K., Hence the different spelling that you might find in the U.S.A.

The Internet has many resources and articles about color blindness, Proptanopia and other forms of color-blindness. The website "color blind awareness" (https://www.colourblindawareness.org) has some fascinating information as do many others sites that deal with this topic.

I highly encourage you to visit some color blindness sites – it's a fun and interesting topic.

# Optical Illusion, Droste, Steganography, Stereograms

Images hidden in images. Several names are used but the concept remains; sometimes we see a "thing" that is not really part of the picture. As old as painting itself, images have been "hidden" or in some cases, just appeared by accident.

The result is endless fascination for those of us that love seeing "things in things." When I started to write "I See Things", I had done no research on the topic. It was more toward the end of writing that I started to wonder about what this is called. After reading a number of articles, I was amazed at how this has been used over the years.

The topic of hidden images is fairly broad and it has a number of branches. One area I find of interest is the logo design. Toyota, FedEx and a fairly large number of iconic brands have hidden images in the corporate logo. Certainly worth a little time on your favorite search engine to read more.

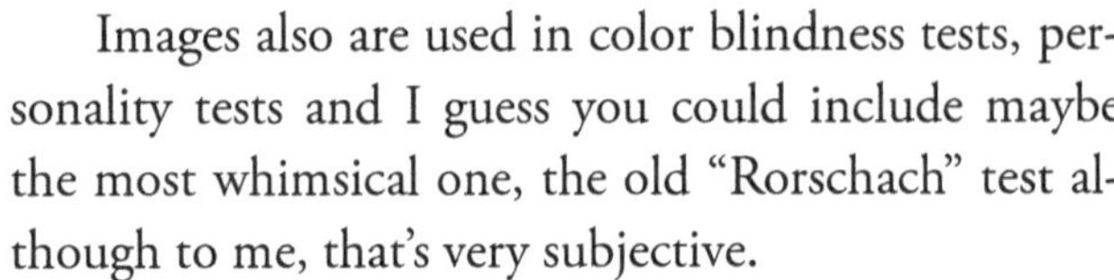

Image credit:
public domain

Images also are used in color blindness tests, personality tests and I guess you could include maybe the most whimsical one, the old "Rorschach" test although to me, that's very subjective.

This image (above) of the young/old woman is a great example of a hidden image. The brain is so good at matching patterns that the computer world is having a hard time figuring out how the brain does it. What we take for granted, a computer program would be extremely difficult to match (if it even could match our brain.)

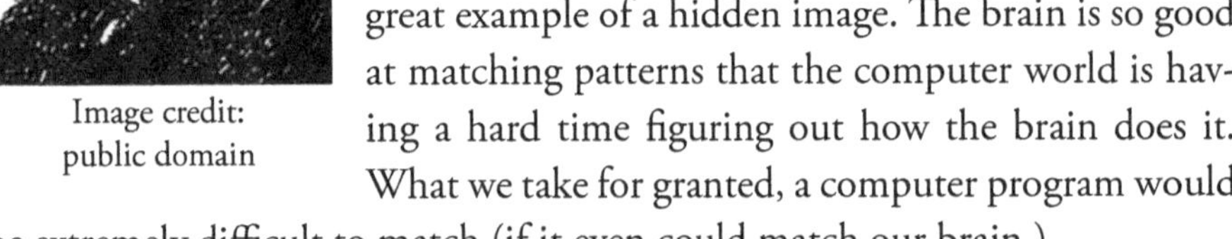

*Lots of material online on this topic. Hope you find it interesting.*

# A Few Thoughts

In my opinion, there is more about life than we will ever know. I can't help but see creatures all around me. Real ones and yes, many imaginary ones. Maybe it's a simple anthropomorphic effect. Maybe not. Still fun to look and wonder if there are more types of living creatures than we know about – When you come right down to it – it's all about perceptions.

*What do you see?*

Perception: "*the state of being or process of becoming aware of something through the senses*" – are we "*aware*" of things?

So, I ask; Do trees have a soul? Does a rock know you are there? At the smallest possible level of matter, does life exist at all?

Who knows… Physicists have probed, measured, tested and theorized for decades and still we have few concrete answers to so many questions. It seems as though the more we look, the more questions we have.

Walking around the woods, cities, beaches, I have to ask this question; "W*hat do I really see and what do I really feel?*"

Have you ever had that "feeling" that someone or "*something*" is looking at you? Have you been alone in the forest and "felt" a presence? I think all of us have had that experience. Sometimes it cannot be explained. It's just a "*feeling.*"

This gets back to the core of *I See Things*. The book is about our perceptions and feelings. It's what happens in my mind and heart. You might have noticed that many pictures are outside. I guess a lot of my time is spent traveling around and enjoying the wonder of this great country.

I hope you wander outside. Take in all the wonder and fascination that our environment offers. I hope *I See things* helps your mind see a little deeper into your world and discover the hidden side of life.

# And Now?

What now? Now it's your turn. Right now, look around you. See anything differently? Walk outside and start looking at those trees in your yard – or the mountains in the distance. Look at the clouds, rocks, and the landscape settings. Every time you look around in your home things will change. The electric plugs seem to be looking at you. Designs in the sheet rock or flooring patterns come to life. They all contain hidden images as do so many things in our lives and all we need to do is look and let our imaginations take over.

At times we all walk through life while thinking about the crazy things we have to do each day. Wake up, get out of bed, shower, get dressed, make breakfast, talk to people, get to work… It's hard to not get caught up with the chores, trials and tribulations of living – but wait! It's amazing what a change in perspective can do to lift us up and give our imagination a chance to bring joy and happiness into our lives. We are surrounded by so many ways to enjoy life that once you let it in, you can't help but smile at the way shapes can change into creatures.

So the baton is being handed over to you – hope you have enjoyed reading "I See Things" and this book has opened your eyes to the possibilities of imagination. Our reality can be harsh and our reality can be fun. I can't know what situation you are in but I can wish and hope that this book has given you new tools and new ways to look at life and all that is around you.

Thank you again for reading *I See Things* and I leave you with this thought:

*"There are times when you must take control of your mind and your thinking or you will miss what is right in front of you"*

Don't spend your life on autopilot – it's all here for you and it's up to you to imagine then create the life you want. Think about it.

Best of luck…

# About the Author

The picture was taken while the author was taking time out from a video project about the famous Jalama Burger in Southern California (*Jalama: Beach to Burgers – available on Amazon.*)

Before his video work, Ric began his professional career playing music in the San Francisco bay area from 1965 until retiring from music in 1980.

After a career in music, it was back to college and high-tech then spending 30 years with technology startups in Seattle, WA. Ric has now returned to writing music and taking on short-form video projects and other creative endeavors like, "I See things."

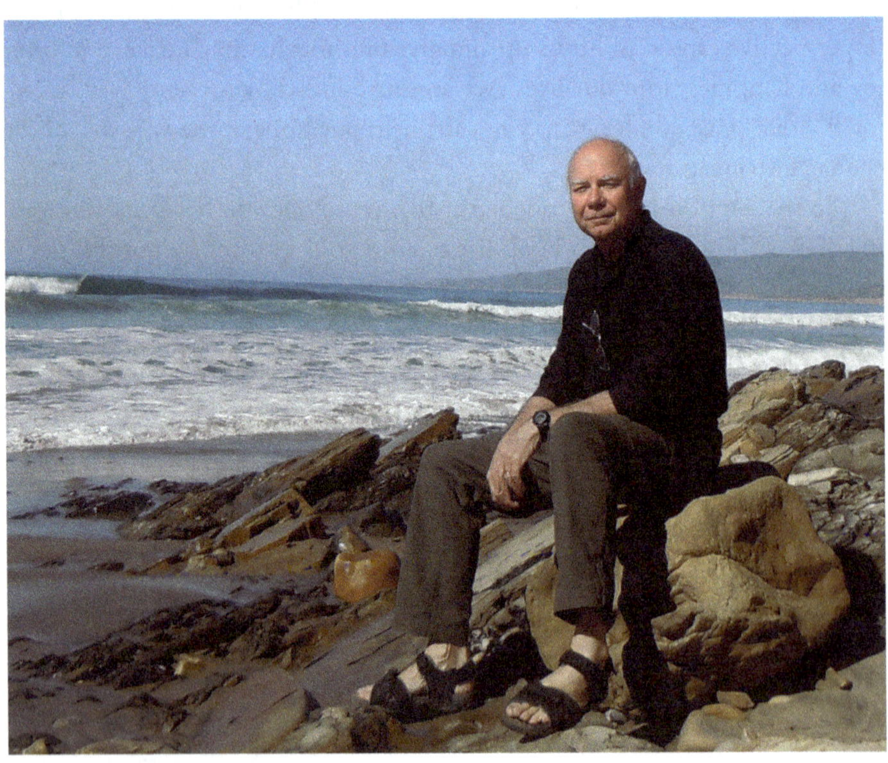

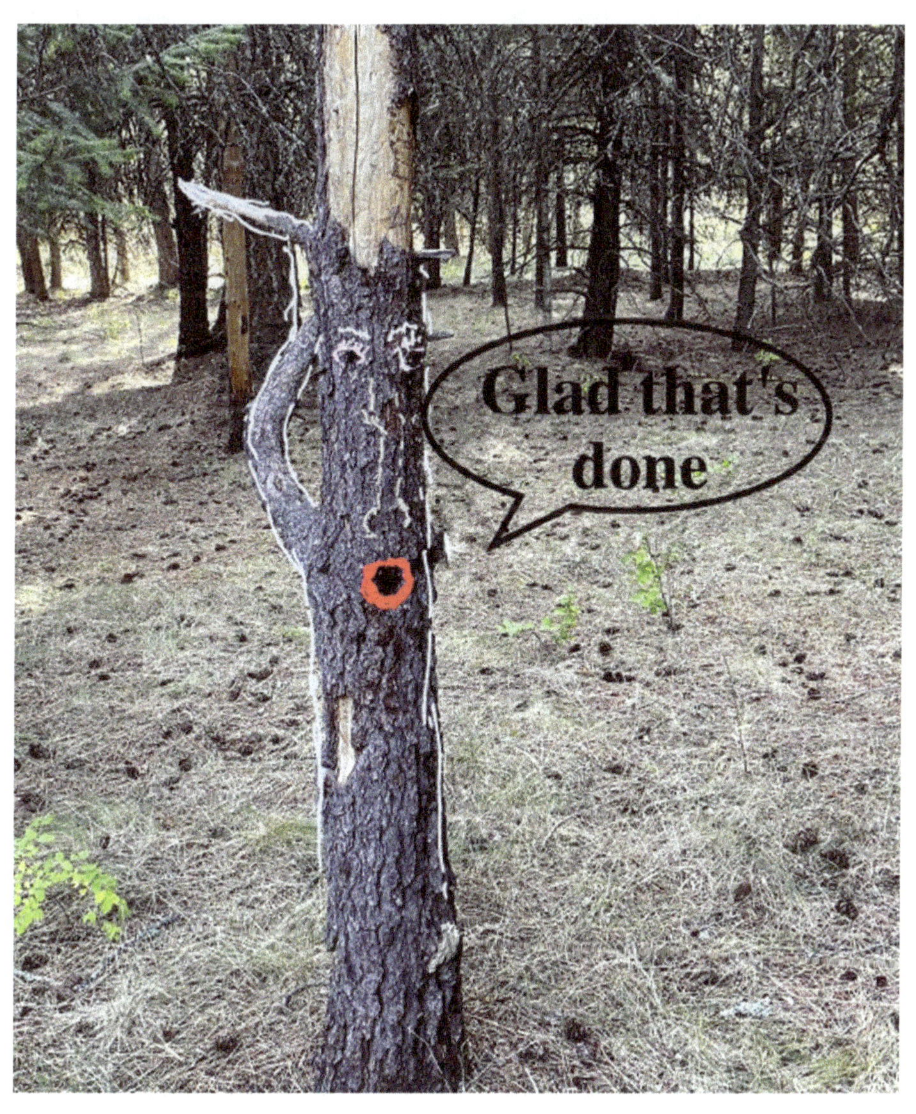


# The End

www.ingramcontent.com/pod-product-compliance
Lightning Source LLC
LaVergne TN
LVHW010837120826
845149LV00017B/1485